Sweet
CHIC

Sweet
CHIC

······· STYLISH TREATS TO DRESS UP FOR ANY OCCASION ·······

Rachel Schifter Thebault

OWNER AND HEAD CONFECTIONER, TRIBECA TREATS

FOREWORD BY ISAAC MIZRAHI

BALLANTINE BOOKS · NEW YORK

For Marin and Sage, the sweetest part of my life

Published in the United States by Ballantine Books,
an imprint of The Random House Publishing Group,
a division of Random House, Inc., New York.

BALLANTINE and colophon are registered trademarks
of Random House, Inc.

Library of Congress Cataloging-in-Publication Data

Thebault, Rachel Schifter.
    Sweet chic : stylish treats to dress up for any
occasion / Rachel Schifter Thebault.
        p.   cm.
    Includes index.
    ISBN 978-0-345-51655-8 (hardcover : alk. paper)
    1. Baking.   I. Title.
TX763.T48 2010
641.8'15—dc22

                                2010014950

Printed in China
on acid-free paper

www.ballantinebooks.com

9 8 7 6 5 4 3 2 1

First Edition

Design by Kris Tobiassen

CONTENTS

Foreword vii

Introduction ix

THE BASICS: From the Runway to Ready-to-Wear. 1

Section One: COOKIES

SCOOPED COOKIES: The White T-shirt 23

THUMBPRINT COOKIES: The Chunky Cardigan 33

VANILLA COOKIES: The Crisp Oxford Shirt 40

CHOCOLATE COOKIES: The Trench Coat 53

BROWNIES: The Cashmere Sweater 66

BUTTERMILK COOKIES: The Pearl Earrings 76

GRAHAM CRACKERS: The Perfect-Fit Jeans 84

Section Two: CAKES

CHOCOLATE CAKE: The Little Black Dress 97

VANILLA CAKE: The A-line Skirt. 113

BANANA CAKE: The Statement Necklace 125

VANILLA ICING: The Ballet Flats 135

CREAM CHEESE ICING: The Navy Blazer. 143

CHOCOLATE ICING: The Knee-High Boots 147

SWISS BUTTERCREAM: The Ruffled Blouse. 154

Section Three: CONFECTIONS

TEMPERED CHOCOLATE: The Stiletto Heels. 162

CHOCOLATE TRUFFLES: The Leather Jacket 171

CARAMEL: The "It" Bag. 181

Acknowledgments. 189

Resources 190

Index 191

Foreword

BY ISAAC MIZRAHI

Style is all about inspiration. When you accessorize an outfit in the right way, it makes you feel great. Lucky for us, Rachel Thebault brings that essential fashion philosophy to delicious, classic desserts with her fabulous debut cookbook, *Sweet Chic*. I mean, why not dress up your favorite cake the same way you accessorize your favorite outfit? The idea of a dessert book that shows you the perfect way to add designer details to classic confections is truly inspired.

If you're anything like me, you have spent hours in the kitchen trying to find the perfect chocolate cake recipe. Now, thanks to Rachel and *Sweet Chic*, you will feel confident dressing that cake for any occasion, from an intimate dinner party to a co-worker's shower to your best friend's birthday soiree. In these pages, Rachel teaches you not only how to master the basics of baking, but how to accessorize your treats to reflect your own personal style. With a little help from Rachel, a traditional Devil's Food Cake becomes a to-die-for Sweet-and-Salty Cake (page 108) or Rocky Road Cupcakes (page 103), and a slab of chocolate transforms into Cranberry Almond Bark (page 167) packed with fruits and nuts or Salt and Pepper Chocolate (page 165).

Rachel's bakery, Tribeca Treats, has been whipping up incredible sweets for my office events for years. The sleek shop, decorated in pinks and browns, exudes downtown cool as the aroma of fresh baked desserts emanates from the open kitchen. And as a guest on my web series, www.watchisaac.com, Rachel showed us how to make her sensational Peanut Butter and Jelly Cupcakes, which, in Tribeca Treats's signature bite-sized portions, not even the dieters in the crowd can resist!

I'm telling you, *Sweet Chic* is so inspiring. It will make you want to break free of tradition and bake things you're excited about. You don't have to stress yourself out to make something fabulous—you have all the tools you need right here. *Hooray!*

ISAAC MIZRAHI

Introduction

Since opening my bakery, Tribeca Treats, in January 2007, I have noticed a distinct pattern. Many of my customers rush in, harried, after work or with kids in tow, needing something last minute for a dinner party, cocktail party, or birthday celebration. They always meant to make something at home, but they either ran out of time or are tired of making the same dessert over and over. I too have experienced this feeling of frustration. Prior to baking professionally, I was an investment banker and now I am a working mother of two, so I know all about time constraints when it comes to baking and entertaining at home.

As the owner of a bakery that focuses on treats for entertaining or gift-giving purposes, I admit that I often benefit from my customers' predicament. But from one busy baker to another, I have walked in your shoes, and I developed this book as a way to help those of you in need and to inspire those of you who bake regularly. My philosophy of baking is simple and comparable to the advice of many fashion experts: Use a little black dress (and a few other staples) as the foundation of your wardrobe and change the accessories to dress it up or down. In a similar way, you can master some basic recipes or techniques and create the foundation for multiple desserts. By making simple alterations to how a base dessert is finished or served, you'll have a complete "wardrobe" of desserts to outfit any occasion.

Take chocolate cake, for example. Typically a cookbook will pair a recipe for the cake with a specific type of icing. You make that recipe once and like it, but then, when you need a cake for a friend who likes darker chocolate, you'll search your cookbooks for another recipe, having no guarantee that an unfamiliar recipe will still be a success. *Sweet Chic* offers one base recipe for a chocolate cake batter and provides alternative baking methods and a variety of icing suggestions. You can now create anything from traditional birthday cake to whimsical mini cupcakes to a romantic cake for two without having to stray from your comfortable cake recipe. The cakes and icings in this book can be mixed and matched in over fifty delectable combinations (see page 96).

Everything in this book is ordered by degree of difficulty. There are three main sections: Cookies are generally easiest to master because they are most resilient to mistakes (such as undercooking or overmixing). Your cakes and icings will be a success once you are comfortable with the basic mixing techniques you learned in the cookies section. Finally, chocolate work requires more finesse than both cookies and cakes, as well as some specialty equipment, so that section appears last in the book.

Each section is divided into chapters that are also ordered by degree of difficulty. For example, the cakes section begins with a Devil's Food Cake base, which can be mixed by hand in one bowl, so that it requires minimal equipment. The icings are grouped separately at the end of the section, with the most simple, Vanilla Icing, kicking those recipes off.

Additionally, all of these recipes in the book can be made, in whole or at least in part, in advance of when you need them. Cookie doughs can be made and then chilled or frozen before they are baked. Cakes can be baked one day and then iced the next. Breaking down recipes into easy-to-follow steps can help immensely as you try to accomplish all your party planning, bits at a time, after work or after you've put the kids to bed.

Sweet Chic aims to make homemade desserts both practical and doable, despite your busy schedule.

LESS IS MORE

At Tribeca Treats, we offer smaller-size desserts so that our customers can satisfy their sweet tooth without overindulging. A plate of elegant cookies or mini cupcakes at the end of a meal goes a long way toward letting your guests linger over conversation and their last glass of wine. Everyone leaves the meal satisfied and happy—especially the successful host!

Many of the recipes in *Sweet Chic* are based on the "small bites" philosophy and are portioned accordingly. In general, the truffles are bite size, the cookies and mini cupcakes are portioned for one or two bites, and the standard cupcakes are portioned to roughly 2½ inches in diameter. Applying this same philosophy in portioning cakes, I recommend cutting them into 1-inch slices for a three-layer cake or 1½-inch slices for a two-layer cake. Using these portions, a three-layer 8-inch cake will feed twenty to twenty-four people.

Keep this in mind when calculating your quantities for serving: I usually recommend two to four chocolates, cookies, or mini cupcakes per guest; one to one and a half standard cupcakes per guest; or one individual dessert or slice of cake per guest.

USE YOUR IMAGINATION

Just as you wouldn't wear clothing only as you saw it worn in a magazine, you aren't expected to make these recipes only one way. These recipes are intended to be used as a guide. Once you are comfortable with standard combinations, you can feel free to mix and match them with other favorite recipes. Each base recipe is like a wardrobe staple that can be worn many different ways and never goes out of style.

I also encourage you to broaden your base of desserts. A wardrobe consists of many different basic elements, not just multiple versions of a little black dress. Similarly, we often learn several different recipes for one dessert (such as the chocolate cake, for example), when our time may be better spent learning a new but similar recipe (such as carrot cake) and just dressing up the chocolate cake differently each time it is served.

At Tribeca Treats and in *Sweet Chic* our signature flavors start with dessert fare classics but are given a sophisticated twist. You'll find childhood favorites such as s'mores or cookies and cream packed into an array of cakes and confections, ranging from basic to more adventurous.

Once a year at the bakery we hold our Cupcake Flavor Competition. Customers submit hundreds of creative suggestions, and they're surprisingly easy to put together. Past winners include the Tiramisù, Rocky Road, Berry Berry Good, and Sassy Pumpkin—all made from simple variations on existing recipes and combinations. While a certain amount of precision is involved in creating the bases for your baked goods, you can really use your imagination with add-ins and finishing touches to create endless varieties of cupcakes, cookies, cakes, and confections.

The recipes in this book are designed for a range of skill levels. Aspiring bakers will be able to practice basic techniques that are common to many pastry recipes and learn to apply them in creating their own dessert varieties. Practiced pastry cooks will be inspired by new ideas on ways to use favorite recipes. It is my hope that no matter what your skill level, you will create a variety of tempting treats and have fun in the process.

The Basics

FROM THE RUNWAY TO READY-TO-WEAR

Adapting the latest runway fashions to your wardrobe is not always easy, but some people seem to be able to pull it off with flair. Professional pastry chefs have a similar knack for creating beautiful, avant-garde desserts that seem impossible to reproduce in a home kitchen. Just as designers may give you a ready-to-wear alternative to haute couture, there are plenty of inventive desserts that you can make at home. In this chapter, you'll find tips on ingredients, equipment, and basic techniques that will help you re-create desserts at a more professional level, yet still make them feel as if they are your own.

Major Ingredients

Most baked goods rely on just a handful of essential ingredients, so the quality of each of these ingredients will noticeably enhance or detract from your final product. In general, I recommend buying fresh, organic eggs and dairy products whenever possible. Make sure your sugar, flour, and other pantry items are stored properly in airtight containers. Don't let your extracts and spices sit on your shelves for too long (try to clean out your cabinet every six months or so). In addition, here are some specifics on frequently used baking ingredients.

BAKING SODA VS. BAKING POWDER Baking soda and baking powder leaven baked goods by causing chemical reactions that form air pockets in batters and doughs. Baking soda, or sodium bicarbonate, reacts immediately when it comes into contact with liquids or acids. Baking powder is baking soda that has been combined with cream of tartar, cornstarch, or other chemical compounds. Double-acting baking powder controls the leavening action of the sodium bicarbonate, allowing it to react initially with other ingredients, but then reacting again with the heat of the oven. Because of this distinction, it is important not to substitute one for the other, as it may cause your baked goods to rise more or less than intended.

CHOCOLATE Chocolate is extremely similar to wine in that the flavor, texture, and overall quality can vary tremendously among manufacturers. The best chocolates will have intense, complex flavors that are influenced by geography, the type of cocoa bean, the roasting process, and the percentage of cocoa solids they contain. Some lower-quality chocolates have additives, such as palm kernel or coconut oil, that can dilute the flavor or give the chocolate a grainy or waxy texture. Premium chocolates are easier to work with when tempering (a process in which chocolate is melted for use in confections). Similarly, dark chocolate is somewhat easier to work with than milk or white chocolate because it has a lower percentage of cocoa butter (white chocolate is technically not chocolate at all, as it is entirely cocoa butter). If you plan on doing a lot of chocolate work, I recommend experimenting with different brands to see which you prefer. At Tribeca Treats our favorites are Valrhona and Michel Cluizel, with Guittard, Cacao Barry, and Callebaut being the slightly more affordable and also very good options. Finally, when storing chocolate, be aware that chocolate is porous and picks up the aromas of nearby ingredients. Pay attention to what you store it near—if the chocolate is close to garlic or onions, it will taste like garlic or onions.

COCOA POWDER Just like good-quality chocolate, good-quality cocoa powder will go a long way in creating a rich chocolate flavor in your desserts. Sometimes you may come across a recipe that calls specifically for Dutch processed (or alkalized) cocoa powder. Unsweetened cocoa powder is naturally very acidic and reacts strongly with baking soda. Dutch processing balances the acidity, making it more neutral and therefore controlling the leavening (though both forms do react with leaveners). Some chefs say alkalized cocoa powder creates a more robust chocolaty dessert. If a recipe doesn't specify, either type can be used.

DAIRY Using a lower-fat version for any dairy ingredient will significantly alter the texture and consistency of your baked goods. Therefore, stick with butter, whole milk, heavy cream, or other ingredients as directed. We use buttermilk in almost all our cake recipes because the enzymes in buttermilk help to break down the glutens in the flour and make for a really soft, moist cake. However, if you can't get buttermilk or don't want to buy a whole quart for one recipe, you can substitute equal parts whole milk and sour cream.

EGGS All our recipes call for large eggs. Eggs should be at room temperature when they are being mixed into butter. Adding cold eggs to nicely softened butter will seize up the mixture and make it harder to emulsify. On the other hand, when separating egg whites, cold eggs are easier to use. For some recipes in this book that call for separated egg whites and where the eggs will be uncooked (such as in royal icing), I like to use preseparated pasteurized egg whites, which can be found in a grocery store. While it is not necessary to use them, doing so is just a good precaution to avoid food-borne contaminants, especially if you are making something for children. When separating your own egg whites, crack the egg in half and either pour the egg into your hand, holding on to the yolk while the egg whites drain through your fingers into a bowl, or pass the yolk back and forth between the two shell halves until all the whites have drained out. Generally, one large egg yields one fluid ounce of egg white.

FLOUR, ALL-PURPOSE VS. CAKE Many cake recipes call for cake flour, which can be hard for home cooks to find. Cake flour has less protein in it and is chlorinated to break down glutens, so it results in a softer, more tender texture, which is desirable in cakes (as compared with the chewier, more elastic texture of bread). Almost all the recipes in this book call for all-purpose flour. When it comes to adding flour to your dough or batter, the key is to not overmix it once you've added it. (Overmixing the flour releases more glutens, which is why you knead bread, but it is not the desired result for cakes or cookies.) In general, these recipes will tell you to mix the flour into your dough or batter on low speed *just* until it's combined.

VANILLA AND OTHER EXTRACTS Using pure rather than imitation extracts will always result in a better-tasting end product. This is particularly true of vanilla extract. There are many great vanilla extracts available, ranging in quality, price, and geographic origin. In recipes calling for vanilla beans, such as our caramel recipe,

using the actual vanilla bean is worth the additional cost. You can also reuse the vanilla bean pods by storing them with granulated sugar in an airtight container. This will impart a vanilla flavor into the sugar and provide an extra oomph when used in your desserts or beverages.

Essential Equipment

If you plan on doing a fair amount of baking at home, I recommend the following equipment.

BRUSHES The most useful brush to have for baking is a standard basting brush, or pastry wet brush. You can use it to brush espresso, simple syrup, or liqueurs onto your cakes or cupcakes, and you can also use it for coating cookies or other pastries with an egg wash.

CAKE PANS Round cake pans are most traditionally used for celebration cakes, and come in a wide range of sizes (8- and 9-inch are used most often). I prefer them to square pans because the cakes come out of the pan more easily and the round sides are easier to ice than a cake with corners. Standard cupcake pans typically have 12 cups with a diameter of 2 inches at the bottom and 2¾ inches at the the top. Mini muffin pans are useful for baking more bite-size treats, and they typically come in trays of 24 1½-inch cups. Silicone "pans" or molds are helpful when making individual frozen desserts (like Ice Cream Sandwiches; see page 60). Regardless of the size or material you choose, having two or three pans of each size will save you time in baking cake layers or cupcakes, but you can always portion batter and bake it one pan at a time, if necessary.

CAKE TURNTABLE While it is not a necessity, a turntable is a helpful investment if you plan on making and decorating lots of your own cakes. You can just as easily place a cake plate on top of an overturned bowl and turn it by hand, but having the actual turntable will allow you to turn it faster and more securely, saving you time and resulting in more smoothly iced cakes.

CANDY THERMOMETERS While not necessary for most day-to-day baking recipes, a candy thermometer is essential for making caramel, as just a few degrees' differential in cooking temperature will result in drastically different consistencies for the caramel. Candy thermometers are also helpful for making brittle, custards, or cooking egg whites, as in the Swiss Buttercream recipe. However, candy thermometers are not used in tempering chocolate, because the chocolate melts at much lower temperatures than are typically found on a candy thermometer scale. For tempering chocolate, a traditional digital kitchen thermometer is most accurate.

ICE CREAM SCOOPS Ice cream scoops, in particular the "trigger" variety, are an extremely helpful tool in portioning cookie dough or cupcake batter. At Tribeca Treats we use them in two sizes—a standard size (2 inches in diameter) that is used to portion cake batter into cupcake wrappers (one scoop per wrapper) and a mini scoop (1¼ inches in diameter, slightly larger than a melon baller) for portioning scooped cookies or mini cupcakes. It makes the baking process extremely efficient, and your treats will have a generally uniform portion size and shape to them. It is important to have the "trigger" type of ice cream scoop because you can easily fill the cavity of the scoop with batter or dough and then drop it cleanly into the wrapper or onto the sheet pan in one smooth motion by squeezing the trigger.

KNIVES Baking doesn't require a lot of specialty knives. A good chef's knife and paring knife will take care of almost everything. A serrated bread knife really comes in handy for trimming cakes, and a rolling pizza cutter is useful for cutting cookie dough or fondant (a sugar dough used in decorating cakes).

OFFSET SPATULA These long metal tools with rounded tips and wooden handles differ from flat spatulas in that the metal part of the tool is bent so that it is offset from the handle by about a half inch. I find the offset version to be more useful than the flat version; it allows you to spread batters, icings, or chocolate without your hand or the handle getting in the way. They come in small and large sizes and are most handy for icing cakes and smoothing batter into pans. They are also useful for chocolate work, especially for spreading ganache and delicately removing freshly dipped truffles from dipping forks.

PARCHMENT PAPER Parchment paper is used for many purposes in baking because it is a nonstick paper that can withstand high temperatures. It's great for lining pans for cookies and cakes, and it is also useful for chocolate work—once it is set, the chocolate will peel easily off the paper. Parchment paper used to be hard to find, but now it can be found in most specialty grocery stores. Alternatively, nonstick cooking sprays, such as Pam, can be used in baking, and waxed paper can be used for chocolate. Silicone mats, sold in specialty kitchen equipment and baking stores, are also handy for baking cookies. On the plus side, they're reusable, but they traditionally fit only sheet pans and won't work for round cakes or smaller square pans.

PASTRY BAGS AND TIPS These finishing tools go a long way to adding style to your sweets. If you use reusable canvas pastry bags, I recommend having three, so that you can cut the ends with different-size openings—one for large tips, one for smaller tips, and one with a very small opening that you can use without a tip at all (for less precise piping needs). Disposable plastic pastry bags are used in the same way as canvas bags, but they should be discarded after one or two uses. As far as tips go, at a minimum, a large round, a large star, and a medium round are helpful tips to have for most basic decorating. Also, small round tips are useful for inscribing cakes and for royal icing work. For more advanced decorating, you can purchase sets of multiple tips and couplers that will cover most of your needs.

ROLLING PINS There are many different rolling pins available. I use a French pin, which is a lightweight wooden pin with tapered ends instead of handles, because it gives me the best control. Whatever the style and material of the rolling pin you choose, the most important thing is to keep it well cleaned and free of scratches, which will cause the dough to stick more easily to the pin. The best way to clean a rolling pin is to wipe it gently but thoroughly with a hot, damp cloth. In situations where you don't have access to a rolling pin, a full or empty wine bottle covered in waxed or parchment paper can be a decent substitute.

RUBBER SPATULA A high-quality, flexible rubber spatula is important to have because it will help you more thoroughly scrape down the sides of your bowl, thus ensuring that the ingredients are well combined. I like the Rubbermaid heat-resistant version that comes in a number of sizes. Bowl scrapers (essentially just hand-size, curved pieces of plastic) can be helpful in emptying bowls, but you won't be able to employ them for as many uses as spatulas because they don't have handles.

SHEET PANS The typical sheet pan (also called a baking sheet) that we use is a 12 x 18-inch aluminum pan with a 1-inch lip all around. (By technical terms this size is a "half" sheet pan. The full sheet pan is generally far too cumbersome for a home cook.) I find this pan to be more versatile than cookie sheets, which don't have fins; it's great for cookies, cakes, chocolate work, and more. I recommend having at least two.

SQUEEZE BOTTLES Squeeze bottles are extremely helpful for garnishing cakes, cupcakes, and other desserts with toppings such as jellies or sauces. Using a bottle to drizzle the jelly or sauce makes adding the finishing touch easy. Also, for the process of flooding decorated cookies with royal icing, as in the Royal Icing Cookies recipe, using a squeeze bottle instead of a pastry bag is much cleaner and easier to control. This is especially true if you are decorating cookies with kids; the sturdier bottles are much less cumbersome than pastry bags for smaller hands. Squeeze bottles can be found at many grocery stores and mass-market retailers (such as Target and Walmart), as well as at many specialty cake supply stores (see Resources, page 190).

STANDING MIXER Although this is a significant investment of money and space, a standing mixer is the one piece of equipment that will truly make your baking life easier. While all the recipes in this book can be mixed by hand, and some are even easier without a mixer, anything with a butter base calls for a standing mixer. Standing mixers typically come with three attachments: a paddle, a whisk, and a dough hook. The dough hook is used primarily for breads, so it is not necessary for any recipe in this book. The whisk is helpful in beating egg whites, so it is called for in the Royal Icing Cookies and Swiss Buttercream recipes. All other recipes that call for a mixer use the paddle attachment. If you are using a handheld mixer or mixing by hand, it is even more important to make sure that all your ingredients start at room temperature, so that you can easily incorporate everything, and be sure to add several minutes of mixing time to each mixing step. All the recipes in this book will fit in a standard 5- or 6-quart mixer.

Basic Techniques

The precision and technique involved in baking often scare people off. With a little practice, however, mastering the fundamentals can be easy, and the more you bake, the more you'll recognize what a perfectly creamed butter or stiff royal icing looks like.

Following are descriptions of these fundamental techniques. I have put them in somewhat chronological order, discussing them as you would use them in a recipe, starting with the most basic steps and then moving into more elaborate skills, such as Icing a Cake or Dipping in Chocolate (see pages 14 and 17). The more you practice these techniques, the easier it will be to pull off exquisite desserts.

PREPARATION All professional kitchens practice a step called "mise en place," a term commonly referring to the process of measuring and preparing all your ingredients before embarking on a recipe. I can't stress enough the importance of this step: It saves time and prevents you from getting to a crucial point in a recipe only to realize that you don't have a key ingredient.

Reading through the recipe before you begin is an important first step. You want to familiarize yourself with the instructions, anticipate any special equipment needed, and understand each stage of the method, such as when you'll need to preheat the oven, bring something to a boil, and so on. Many of these recipes also require at least one hour of chilling time, or other breaks in the flow of work. It is helpful to anticipate these, so that you leave yourself enough time and don't end up rushing the process.

When measuring your ingredients, all liquids need to be measured with a liquid measuring cup (like the glass Pyrex kind). The volume of liquid and nonliquid cups differs slightly, and using the same measure for both can alter the result of the recipe. Dry ingredients and sugar should be measured with a "scoop and sweep" method: Scoop the ingredient into your measuring cup, then sweep your finger or a spatula across the top to level it to the rim of the cup. With the exception of brown sugar, never pack an ingredient into the cup. Recipes are written for the scoop and sweep method, and packing will change the volume added. Finally, unless otherwise noted, be sure butter and eggs are at room temperature. Cold butter will remain lumpy, and cold eggs will cause smooth butter to seize up.

SIFTING FLOUR Sifting flour is important because it removes any lumps in the flour and is the best way to ensure that you won't be biting into any pockets of unincorporated flour in your final product.

Sifting all other dry ingredients (baking soda/powder, cocoa powder, spices, salt) along with the flour will help them to be evenly incorporated into your batter or dough. (Note that sugar is not considered a dry ingredient; because it melts and dissolves into liquid, it acts like a liquid in baking. Measure and add sugar separately from the dry ingredients unless a recipe specifies otherwise.) Finally, sifting adds air to the mixture, which will give you a lighter, fluffier product.

Flour and other dry ingredients should be measured before they are sifted, using the "scoop and sweep" method (see above). However, if you don't have the time or equipment to sift the flour, there is an alternative. Measure all your dry ingredients into a large mixing bowl. Use a wire whisk to gently stir and aerate the flour and other ingredients, making sure to look for lumps of flour and work them out.

CREAMING BUTTER In most of these cake and cookie recipes, it is important to beat the butter so that it is completely smooth and noticeably paler before moving on to the next steps. I recommend about three minutes, unless otherwise indicated. Once you start to add other ingredients, it will be virtually impossible to eliminate any lumps of butter.

After you do add other ingredients, be sure to thoroughly scrape down the bottom and sides of your mixing bowl with a rubber spatula between each addition. Otherwise, you'll realize too late that you have chunks of butter or pockets of flour that never got fully incorporated.

ROLLING DOUGH Rolling out cookie dough can be time consuming and arduous, but with some practice you can easily get the technique down.

After you make cookie dough, you will divide it and shape it into flat disks (1 to 2 inches thick) before chilling it for at least 1 hour, or until it is firm. When you remove a disk from the refrigerator, it may initially be too firm to start rolling. If the dough cracks or breaks apart when you try to roll it, then you will need to let it warm up slightly. Pounding it lightly with a rolling pin will help soften it as well. The dough is ready to roll when it flattens and spreads without cracking but is not so soft that it sticks to the rolling pin.

To begin rolling, lightly dust your work surface and the dough with flour. (Alternatively, the dough can be rolled between two pieces of parchment or waxed paper.) Place the rolling pin in the center of the disk and push outward, flattening half the dough away from your body. Do not push the rolling pin back and forth, because this will cause the dough to spread and retract, making the process take longer and overworking the dough. Also be careful of pushing too hard on the edges as the pin rolls off the sides of the dough. This will cause the edges of your dough to be rolled thinner than the center.

After each push, rotate the dough about 45 degrees and then repeat, rolling from the center. Dust lightly with more flour if the dough starts to stick to the work surface or rolling pin. (If you are rolling the dough between two pieces of parchment or waxed paper, peel both the top and bottom layers of paper away from the dough between each rotation. This will prevent the paper from wrinkling against the dough as you roll it out.) Continue rotating the dough and rolling it until you have reached the desired thickness. Check that the dough is even, and level it, if necessary, with a couple more gentle rolls.

Dough should be rolled to a little more than ¼ inch thick for larger sugar cookies and slightly thinner for ice cream sandwich cookies. For small sandwich cookies, dough should be rolled to a thickness of about ⅛ inch. The unused portions of dough after it has been cut can be gathered and rerolled two or three times. After that, the dough becomes overworked and must be discarded, or it can be baked off and ground into crumbs and reserved for other uses, such as cake and ice cream toppings. Cookie dough can be frozen either before or after it is cut.

I recommend making a double batch of rolled cookie dough each time you prepare it. This way, you can keep the extra prerolled dough in the freezer, and the next time you want to make cookies, all the hard work is done. Keep the prerolled dough on a sheet pan (with any layers of dough separated with parchment or waxed paper) and wrap it with at least two layers of plastic wrap to freeze. If a sheet pan will not fit in your freezer, using a paring knife, cut the chilled dough into a smaller size and stack layers of rolled dough with parchment or waxed paper on the bottom and in between, then wrap the stack with at least two layers of plastic wrap. When wrapped tightly, cookie dough can be kept in the freezer for up to 8 weeks.

FILLING A PASTRY BAG AND PIPING If you frequently decorate cakes or cupcakes, have a few reusable canvas pastry bags in your kitchen. (I often multipurpose mine to make savory hors d'oeuvres or canapés.) Disposable plastic pastry bags are also available through most specialty cake or kitchen supply stores, and, in a pinch, cutting off one corner of a large resealable plastic freezer bag can also do the trick. You should also have several tips on hand for a variety of purposes (see Pastry Bags and Tips, page 6). In some of these recipes, you may be instructed to use a pastry bag with no tip. For this instruction you'll want the opening of the bag to be no larger than ¼ inch, so if you are using canvas bags and the ends are cut with a wider hole, use a small or medium round tip along with the bag.

To Assemble the Bag and Tip: If your pastry bag is unused, cut an opening at the tip of the bag. The opening should be just big enough to allow the narrow end of the tip or coupler to fit entirely through, but small enough that the wider end cannot be squeezed through the hole. Place the tip inside the bag and position it with the narrow end of the tip coming through the opening of the bag.

To Fill the Bag: Fold the wide edge of the bag down about 3 inches and fit one hand beneath the fold so that you can grasp the bag in that hand. Using a rubber spatula, scoop the icing into the bag, gently shaking the bag after each scoop and nudging the icing to settle toward the bottom. Fill the bag so that the icing comes 1 to 2 inches from where the bag is folded. Unfold the top edge and, starting from the wide edge of the bag, squeeze the icing toward the tip and remove any air bubbles (imagine squeezing the last bit of toothpaste toward the end of a toothpaste tube). Twist the wide end of the bag to just above where the icing has settled. Note that the more filled a pastry bag is, the harder it will be to control. For precise work, such as for cake inscriptions and royal icing, you may want to fill the bag with just a half cup of icing at a time and refill as necessary.

To Pipe: Grasp the twisted part of the bag in the crux of your thumb and forefinger on your dominant hand. The palm of your hand should be resting on the most bulbous part of the bag and be able to gently squeeze the bag from the top of the icing. Use your nondominant hand to guide the tip. Hold the tip perpendicular to the surface of the cake or cookie when piping.

For Royal Icing Cookies: Royal icing is used in two consistencies, stiff and flood. The stiff form is the initial result of a royal icing recipe. You can use it to outline the borders of your cookie and add any details such as words and other design elements, because it doesn't spread after you pipe it and generally hardens quickly. Adding small amounts of water to the stiff icing results in the "flood." The flood literally floods the cookie with icing up to where you have piped a border with the stiff icing. It takes longer to dry fully (about twelve hours), but it results in a smooth, hard coating over the surface of the cookie.

Trace the outline of the cookie by piping the icing along the edges. Work slowly so that the icing doesn't stretch or break. If an air bubble causes the icing to break, either fill in the gap by piping icing in between or scrape it off and begin again. When forming corners, drop the tip to almost meet the surface, creating a hinge, and continue to pipe in the new direction. When you get back to the starting point, drop the tip again to meet the icing where it began, then stop squeezing and pull up gently but swiftly. Once the outline has set, you'll be able to fill in the center with your flood. To flood the cookies, use a squeeze bottle or pastry bag to fill the spaces within the outline with the thinner royal icing (see Royal Icing Cookies, page 49).

For Cupcakes: Whether you use a round or star tip, a rosette shape (a spiral pattern) is the best way to cover the surface of a standard-size cupcake. Start with the tip near the edge of the top of the cupcake. Begin drawing a circle around the edge and when you reach where you started, spiral the icing in toward the middle. Once the surface of the cupcake is covered, release the pressure on the bag and gently pull up the tip.

For Mini Cupcakes and Cake Borders: To pipe stars or dots (which make nice borders for cakes or, when piped slightly larger, are an elegant way to frost a mini cupcake), use a large star or round tip and hold the tip of the bag perpendicular to the surface. Squeeze softly until the icing is as wide as you want it, then release the pressure and gently pull up the tip.

ICING A CAKE One of the most important steps in icing a cake is trimming the cake layers evenly, as flat, even layers will allow you to stack a level cake. Take a serrated knife and, holding it with the blade parallel to the work surface, shave the top of the cake by turning the cake as you slowly cut in from the edge, keeping the knife level. Remove the top of the cake and discard (or reserve for another recipe to make crumbs). Ideally, each cake layer should be trimmed to equal height—about 1 inch thick for a three-layer cake or 1½ inches thick for two layers.

To begin icing the cake, make sure the cake layers are chilled or completely cooled to room temperature. Place one layer on a cake plate or cardboard round (available at specialty cake supply stores; see Resources, page 190) bottom side

Icing a Cake

1   2   3

4   5   6

down. Scoop the icing onto the layer with an offset spatula and spread it toward the edges with the spatula. Keep adding icing until the layer of icing is about ½ inch thick and it reaches just past the edges of the cake all around. Take the next layer and fit it on top (again, bottom side down), gently pressing it into the icing once it is centered. Repeat by spreading more icing on top, to about ½ inch thick, but this time focus on making sure that the cake appears level, using more or less icing in parts to flatten the surface. Add the top layer of cake, this time placing the side that was at the bottom of the pan up, because it is flatter and will be smoother for icing the top. Once that layer is centered, gently press it into the icing underneath.

Once all the layers are assembled, you will create a "crumb coat" around the outside of the cake. The crumb coat is a thin layer of icing that seals the cake layers before the final coat of icing, preventing any crumbs from showing up in the outer layer. It is also the best opportunity for you to get the cake as flat and smooth as you want. Working with this thinner layer of icing is easier than with the thicker final layer, so take your time and spread a thin layer of icing all around the top and sides of the cake. Fill in any gaps in the cake with extra icing, and shape the cake so that the sides and top are flat. Refrigerate the cake for about 30 minutes to allow the crumb coat to set.

Finally, apply the final outer layer of icing (¼ to ½ inch thick) to the cake. Pipe a border around the top and bottom edges of the cake, if desired.

Adding a layer of "striping" to a cake is achieved by spreading a thin layer of jelly or ganache over the interior layers of cake, before adding the icing. Spread it on each cake layer as if you were spreading jelly on a slice of bread. If the jelly is spread thinly enough, it will adhere to the cake, and when you add the icing on top, it will remain a distinct layer. Striping your cake is a great way to add a subtle bit of extra flavor to the cake.

DOUBLE BOILING Many pastry ingredients, such as chocolate or egg whites, are too delicate to be exposed to the direct heat of a stove top. Therefore, when you need to melt or heat them, it is best to use a double boiling method. No special equipment is necessary. Just bring a saucepan or pot of water to a low boil and place your ingredients in a glass or ceramic mixing bowl set above the boiling water. The bowl should be wider than the pan, so it can rest on the rim without falling inside. (A metal bowl can also be used, but since metal conducts heat faster, it is important to stir vigorously, so that your mixture doesn't burn on the edges. Try to keep the boiling water from rising up to make direct contact with the bowl, and stir continuously to evenly expose the ingredients to the heated area.

Dipping in Chocolate

1   2   3

DIPPING IN CHOCOLATE Many of the recipes in this book call for a cookie or confection to be dipped in chocolate as a finishing touch. "Tempered" chocolate is achieved in a process whereby you melt the chocolate to certain temperatures in order to optimize the molecular configuration of the chocolate (see Tempered Chocolate, page 162). Properly tempered chocolate sets extremely quickly and produces a beautiful sheen on the finished product. For that reason, tempering chocolate is a necessity in most recipes where you will be coating something with chocolate or otherwise melting and then resetting the chocolate. Tempered Chocolate: The Stiletto Heels discusses how to properly temper chocolate, but until you have learned how to do so, or if you just want to save time, there is a shortcut. Add 1 tablespoon vegetable or canola oil per 2 cups chopped chocolate that you are melting and you will be able to achieve a smoothly melted chocolate that won't "bloom." (Blooming is when the fat or sugar crystals in the chocolate separate, causing a discoloration. Bloomed chocolate is perfectly fine to eat; it just looks unattractive.) The oil does, however, dilute the flavor of the chocolate slightly, so, if you are able to, it is preferable to properly temper it in most cases.

When using the oil method, mix the oil and chocolate together in a bowl and then melt them over a double boiler or in a microwave, heating them in 30-second increments. (Because you have less control with the microwave, the double boiling method is preferable until you are comfortable with recognizing the proper consistency in melted chocolate.)

Regardless of the method you use to heat the chocolate, be careful not to burn it. (You can tell that it is burned if the chocolate starts to form small bubbles on the sides of the bowl. If any part of the chocolate has burned, the entire batch is unusable, as the chocolate will never fully harden again.) Stir the chocolate constantly as you melt it and look for it to get to the point where it is a thick, viscous liquid (about the consistency of buttermilk or heavy cream) with some bits of solid remaining. Stop heating it and stir until the remaining solids have melted into the mixture.

Once your chocolate has fully melted, let it cool slightly (for about 1 minute) and then you can begin to use it. Work quickly so that the chocolate in the bowl doesn't set before you finish. (If it does set, you can still remelt it using the original melting method.) If you are fully enrobing a treat (for example, a cookie), use a chocolate dipping fork, a small offset spatula, or a regular fork with long tines. Balance the cookie on the fork or spatula and dip it entirely into the chocolate, until it is fully immersed. If the cookie falls off the fork or spatula into the chocolate, just scoop it up and try to regain control as you lift it out of the chocolate. If you are dipping something that will not be fully enrobed, just hold the part that will not be covered as you dip it into the chocolate.

When you remove the cookie from the chocolate, gently shake it to get rid of the excess chocolate. Then, pull it out of the bowl, lightly scraping the fork, spatula, or cookie against the rim of the bowl to remove even more excess chocolate from the bottom. Place it on a sheet pan covered in parchment or waxed paper and allow it to set. Repeat with the remaining items.

Ideally, anything dipped in chocolate should be able to set at room temperature. However, if you need something more quickly, or if you are working in a warm room, you can allow it to set in the refrigerator. Be careful not to refrigerate chocolate for too long, however, as the humidity from the refrigerator will affect the appearance of the chocolate by causing it to bloom.

Making It Last

While freshly made treats are typically preferable, many desserts stand up remarkably well to freezing, which can be an important time-saver. The most important thing to remember about freezing is to make sure that anything you freeze is wrapped well and airtight to prevent freezer burn. Cookie doughs (primarily the scooped cookies and Vanilla and Chocolate Cookie doughs) are the best desserts in this book to freeze. Most can be finished up to the point of baking and then frozen, and next time you want fresh-baked cookies, they can be ready in less than 20 minutes and without the usual mess. The brownies in this book can be frozen after they are baked and thawed before serving (overnight in the refrigerator or for about 3 hours at room temperature).

Cake layers can be frozen after they are baked and before they are iced. I recommend trimming the tops first (see Icing a Cake, page 14) and making sure that the cakes have cooled entirely before wrapping them in plastic wrap (any steam left in the cake will cause ice crystals to form on the cake). Freezing cake layers is a practice commonly used by wedding cake bakers and anyone else who needs to begin assembling and decorating a large cake in advance of when it will be served. While it is also possible to freeze a cake after it's iced, it can sometimes be hit or miss with the icing, so I don't recommend it.

Finally, ganache, when it is being used to make truffles, can also be frozen. Cut the ganache into the shape of the truffles, but before you dip the truffles, wrap them in an airtight container (such as Tupperware) or wrap them on a sheet pan with at least two layers of plastic wrap to freeze. Let them thaw in the refrigerator overnight, then dip them in tempered chocolate. Be sure to remove any perspiration that may have accumulated on the ganache by dabbing gently with a paper towel before you dip them in tempered chocolate (any water will bring chocolate out of temper and cause it to bloom).

SECTION ONE

Cookies

Cookies are similar to the most accessible items in your wardrobe: your everyday and weekend wear. They make a good foundation for beginner baking. Though maybe not as celebratory as some other items, cookies are a reliable go-to for an everyday snack, a weekend at a vacation home, and even a dressier occasion now and then. Once you feel comfortable mastering the techniques of cookies, you'll be able to pull off even more stylish numbers with ease.

Scooped Cookies

THE WHITE T-SHIRT
············

* **CHOCOLATE CHIP COOKIES**
* **White Chocolate Coconut Cookies**
* **Oatmeal Raisin Cookies**
* **Snickerdoodles**

Just like a white T-shirt, the chocolate chip cookie is about as basic as you can get. A casual staple that can easily be dressed up with the right accompaniments, scooped cookies are perfect for an after-school snack or movie-night nosh, but they can also be a popular late-night treat at a sweet sixteen party or other big event.

I call this category of cookies "scooped cookies" because the dough is portioned out (literally scooped) into balls before baking. I suggest using a mini ice cream scoop (1¼ inches in diameter) to form the dough balls because it makes for small, even-size cookies. Scoop these cookies into balls and then freeze them—you can bake them straight out of the freezer (just add a few minutes to the cooking time), and they make an easy treat for unexpected guests or a comforting midnight snack.

Chocolate Chip Cookies

MAKES ABOUT 3 DOZEN COOKIES

Chocolate chip cookies should be the basis for anyone's foray into baking. They are simple to make, an all-time favorite, and extremely versatile. Portioned on the smaller side, these cookies can make for a satisfying end to a dinner party or a welcome thank-you gift.

The spectrum of chocolate chip cookies is wide, with personal favorites ranging from thin and crispy to soft and chewy. This particular recipe results in a cookie on the softer, more cakey side. It is important to chill the dough thoroughly, for at least one hour, before scooping and baking these cookies. If the dough is too soft when it goes into the oven, the cookie will spread and be very thin.

1 **cup all-purpose flour**
¼ **teaspoon baking soda**
¼ **teaspoon salt**
8 **tablespoons (1 stick) unsalted butter, at room temperature**
⅓ **cup packed light brown sugar**
⅓ **cup granulated sugar**
1 **large egg, at room temperature**
2 **teaspoons pure vanilla extract**
¾ **cup mini semisweet chocolate chips**

1. Sift the flour, baking soda, and salt into a mixing bowl and set aside.

2. Beat the butter in the bowl of a standing mixer fitted with a paddle attachment at high speed until it is light and fluffy, about 3 minutes.

3. Add the brown and granulated sugars, crumbling the brown sugar with your hands as you add it to get rid of any lumps. Mix on medium-high speed until smooth, about 1 minute. Scrape down the sides and bottom of the bowl with a rubber spatula halfway through mixing to ensure that the butter and sugar are well mixed.

4. Add the egg and vanilla and mix until combined. Again, scrape down the sides and bottom of the bowl to make sure that the ingredients are incorporated.

5. Add approximately half the flour mixture and mix on low speed just until the flour is incorporated, about 30 seconds. Repeat with the remaining flour and scrape down the sides and bottom of the bowl to ensure that the flour is fully incorporated.

6. Stir in the chocolate chips and mix just until combined, about 10 seconds. Remove the dough from the bowl, press it into a flat mound, and wrap it in plastic wrap. Let it chill in the refrigerator for at least 1 hour or up to 3 days.

7. While the dough is chilling, preheat the oven to 350°F. Line two sheet pans with parchment paper or spray lightly with nonstick cooking spray.

8. Remove the chilled dough from the refrigerator and scoop or roll it into balls about 1 tablespoon in size. At this point, the cookie dough can be frozen in an airtight container for up to 1 month (separate layers of dough balls with waxed paper).

9. Place the balls of dough about 1 inch apart on the prepared pans. Bake for 12 to 15 minutes, rotating the pans once halfway through, until the edges of the cookies are golden brown. Remove the cookies from the oven, let them cool slightly, then transfer them to a wire rack to cool to room temperature (or serve warm).

10. Keep the cookies in an airtight container at room temperature for up to 4 days.

POLISH YOUR LOOK Traditional chocolate chip cookies incorporate semisweet chocolate chips, but if you prefer milk chocolate, feel free to substitute. If you like nuts in your chocolate chip cookies, add ½ cup chopped walnuts or other nuts.

White Chocolate Coconut Cookies

MAKES ABOUT 3 DOZEN COOKIES

This cookie is a simple variation of Chocolate Chip Cookies (page 24). By switching out the chocolate chips for white chocolate and coconut, you get something a little more exotic. Play around with this base cookie dough and change up the flavor with a variety of different mix-ins. This particuar recipe goes well with tropical themes or summery occasions.

- 1 **cup all-purpose flour**
- ¼ **teaspoon baking soda**
- ¼ **teaspoon salt**
- 8 **tablespoons (1 stick) unsalted butter, at room temperature**
- ⅓ **cup packed light brown sugar**
- ⅓ **cup granulated sugar**
- 1 **large egg, at room temperature**
- 2 **teaspoons pure vanilla extract**
- ½ **cup white chocolate chips**
- ½ **cup unsweetened shredded coconut**

1. Sift the flour, baking soda, and salt into a mixing bowl and set aside.

2. Beat the butter in the bowl of a standing mixer fitted with the paddle attachment at high speed until it is light and fluffy, about 3 minutes.

3. Add the brown and granulated sugars, crumbling the brown sugar with your hands as you add it to get rid of any lumps. Mix on medium-high speed until smooth, about 1 minute. Scrape down the sides and bottom of the bowl with a rubber spatula halfway through mixing to ensure that the butter and sugar are well mixed.

4. Add the egg and vanilla and mix until combined. Again, scrape down the sides and bottom of the bowl to make sure that the ingredients are incorporated.

5. Add approximately half the flour mixture and mix on low speed just until the flour is incorporated, about 30 seconds. Repeat with the remaining flour and scrape down the sides and bottom of the bowl to ensure that the flour is fully incorporated.

6. Stir in the white chocolate and coconut and mix just until combined, about 10 seconds. Remove the dough from the bowl, press it into a flat mound, and wrap it in plastic wrap. Let it chill in the refrigerator for at least 1 hour or up to 3 days.

7. While the dough is chilling, preheat the oven to 350°F. Line two sheet pans with parchment paper or spray lightly with nonstick cooking spray.

8. Remove the chilled dough from the refrigerator and scoop or roll it into balls about 1 tablespoon in size. At this point, the cookie dough can be frozen in an airtight container for up to 1 month (separate layers of dough balls with waxed paper).

9. Place the balls of dough about 1 inch apart on the prepared pans. Bake for 12 to 15 minutes, rotating the pans once halfway through, until the edges of the cookies are golden brown. Remove the cookies from the oven, let them cool slightly, then transfer them to a wire rack to cool to room temperature (or serve warm).

10. Keep the cookies in an airtight container at room temperature for up to 4 days.

POLISH YOUR LOOK For another popular flavor combination, reduce the coconut to ¼ cup and add ¼ cup chopped macadamia nuts, or substitute macadamia nuts for all the coconut. To evoke fall flavors, add 1 teaspoon ground cinnamon and use dried fruit (such as cranberries or chopped apricots) instead of the coconut. Or, for another everyday version, use ½ cup butterscotch chips and ½ cup chopped pecans. Just keep in mind the ratio of dough to mix-ins (about ¾ to 1 cup mix-ins per recipe) and experiment!

Oatmeal Raisin Cookies

MAKES ABOUT 3 DOZEN COOKIES

This cookie is a slightly different base recipe from the chocolate chip cookie recipes, but the basic technique is the same. The brown sugar and oats are the most noticeable flavors in this chewy cookie. For a crunchier version that highlights the raisins more, add 2 to 4 minutes to the cooking time. You can also play around with this recipe by adding semisweet chocolate chips or dried cranberries (or both) instead of raisins.

1	**cup all-purpose flour**
½	**teaspoon baking soda**
½	**teaspoon salt**
8	**tablespoons (1 stick) unsalted butter, at room temperature**
¾	**cup packed light brown sugar**
1	**large egg, at room temperature**
½	**teaspoon pure vanilla extract**
1½	**cups rolled oats**
¾	**cup raisins**

1. Sift the flour, baking soda, and salt into a mixing bowl and set aside.

2. Beat the butter in the bowl of a standing mixer fitted with a paddle attachment at high speed until it is light and fluffy, about 3 minutes.

3. Add the brown sugar, crumbling it with your hands as you add it to get rid of any lumps. Mix on medium-high speed until smooth, about 1 minute. Scrape down the sides and bottom of the bowl with a rubber spatula halfway through mixing to ensure that the butter and sugar are well mixed.

4. Add the egg and vanilla and mix until combined. Again, scrape down the sides and bottom of the bowl to make sure that the ingredients are incorporated.

5. Add approximately half the flour mixture and mix on low speed just until the flour is incorporated, about 30 seconds. Repeat with the remaining flour and scrape down the sides and bottom of the bowl to ensure that the flour is fully incorporated.

6. Add the oats and raisins and mix just until combined, about 20 seconds. Remove the dough from the bowl, press it into a flat mound, and wrap it in plastic wrap. Let it chill in the refrigerator for at least 1 hour or up to 3 days.

7. While the dough is chilling, preheat the oven to 350°F. Line two sheet pans with parchment paper or spray lightly with nonstick cooking spray.

8. Remove the chilled dough from the refrigerator and scoop or roll it into balls about 1 tablespoon in size. At this point, the cookie dough can be frozen in an airtight container for up to 1 month (separate layers of dough balls with waxed paper).

9. Place the balls of dough about 1 inch apart on the prepared pans. Bake for 12 to 15 minutes, rotating the pans once halfway through, until the edges of the cookies are golden brown. If you're baking them straight from the freezer, gently press the tops of the cookies with an offset spatula when you rotate them halfway through, so they spread a little. Remove the cookies from the oven, let them cool slightly, then transfer them to a wire rack to cool to room temperature (or serve warm).

10. Keep the cookies in an airtight container at room temperature for up to 4 days.

Snickerdoodles

MAKES ABOUT 3 DOZEN COOKIES

This simple, buttery cinnamon sugar cookie—crispy around the edges and chewy in the middle—is one of our most popular cookies at Tribeca Treats. Despite the sugar coating, the butter and salt offset the sweetness, giving the cookie a nice balance of flavors. For a more traditional sugar cookie, you can leave out the cinnamon and coat the cookie with only sugar.

Snickerdoodles bake to form a perfectly round, flat shape, so they make a beautiful, simple holiday gift stacked in a cellophane bag and tied with a ribbon.

1½ **cups all-purpose flour**
1 **teaspoon cream of tartar**
½ **teaspoon baking soda**
½ **teaspoon salt**
8 **tablespoons (1 stick) unsalted butter, at room temperature**
¾ **cup plus 2 tablespoons sugar**
1 **large egg, at room temperature**
1 **tablespoon ground cinnamon**

1. Sift the flour, cream of tartar, baking soda, and salt into a mixing bowl and set aside.

2. Beat the butter in the bowl of a standing mixer fitted with a paddle attachment at high speed until it is light and fluffy, about 3 minutes.

3. Add ¾ cup sugar and mix on medium-high speed until smooth, about 1 minute. Scrape down the sides and bottom of the bowl with a rubber spatula halfway through mixing to ensure that the butter and sugar are well mixed.

4. Add the egg and mix until combined. Again, scrape down the sides and bottom of the bowl to make sure that the ingredients are incorporated.

5. Add approximately half the flour mixture and mix on low speed just until the flour is incorporated, about 30 seconds. Repeat with the remaining flour and scrape down the sides and bottom of the bowl to ensure the flour is fully incorporated.

6. Remove the dough from the bowl and wrap it in plastic wrap. Let it chill in the refrigerator for at least 1 hour or up to 3 days.

7. While the dough is chilling, preheat the oven to 350°F. Line two sheet pans with parchment paper or spray lightly with nonstick cooking spray.

8. Remove the chilled dough from the refrigerator and scoop or roll it into balls about 1 tablespoon in size. At this point, the cookie dough can be frozen in an airtight container for up to 1 month (separate layers of dough balls with waxed paper).

9. When ready to bake, mix 2 tablespoons sugar with the cinnamon in a small bowl. Roll each ball of dough gently in the bowl to coat with the cinnamon sugar mixture.

10. Place the balls of dough about 1 inch apart on the prepared pans. Bake for 12 to 15 minutes, rotating the pans once halfway through, until the edges of the cookies are firm (the cookies will remain fairly light in color). Remove the cookies from the oven, let them cool slightly on the pans, then transfer them to a wire rack to cool to room temperature (or serve warm).

11. Keep the cookies in an airtight container at room temperature for up to 4 days.

Thumbprint Cookies

THE CHUNKY CARDIGAN

．．．．．．．．．．．．．．．．．

✳ **PEANUT BUTTER AND CHOCOLATE THUMBPRINTS**

✳ **Linzer Thumbprints**

✳ **Chocolate Amaretto Thumbprints**

Thumbprint cookies make you feel cozy and are texturally pleasing to the eye, just like a soft, thick cable-knit sweater. In the same way that a cardigan adds an extra layer to any outfit, thumbprint cookies add an extra element of flavor to a traditional bite-size sweet. These cookies will make a great impression (no pun intended) on your guests: The simple addition of a flavor-filled center suggests that the cookies took more effort to make than they actually required.

Like scooped cookies, these cookies can be prepared up to the point you're ready to bake them and then the dough can be frozen for up to 8 weeks. That way, you've done most of the work ahead of time, though, unlike the scooped cookies, you will have one last step of filling the thumbprints once they are baked.

Peanut Butter and Chocolate Thumbprints

MAKES ABOUT 3 DOZEN COOKIES

This thumbprint cookie marries chocolate and peanut butter in an especially pleasing way. The base of this cookie is similar to a traditional peanut butter cookie, but where other peanut butter cookies tend to be on the drier side, the ganache filling in this one helps give it a moist texture.

1½ **cups all-purpose flour**
½ **teaspoon salt**
8 **tablespoons (1 stick) unsalted butter, at room temperature**
½ **cup packed light brown sugar**
1 **teaspoon pure vanilla extract**
2 **tablespoons whole milk**
¼ **cup creamy peanut butter**

FOR THE FILLING

1 **cup milk chocolate chips or chopped milk chocolate**
1 **tablespoon light corn syrup**
1 **teaspoon pure vanilla extract**
1 **tablespoon heavy cream**
1 **tablespoon creamy peanut butter**

1. Sift the flour and salt together into a mixing bowl and set aside.

2. Beat the butter in the bowl of a standing mixer fitted with a paddle attachment at high speed until it is light and fluffy, about 3 minutes.

3. Add the brown sugar, crumbling it with your hands as you add it to get rid of any lumps. Mix on medium-high speed until smooth, about 1 minute. Scrape down the sides and bottom of the bowl with a rubber spatula halfway through mixing to ensure that the butter and sugar are well mixed.

4. Add the vanilla and mix until combined. Again, scrape down the sides and bottom of the bowl to make sure that the ingredients are incorporated.

5. Add approximately half the flour mixture and mix on low speed just until the flour is incorporated, about 30 seconds. Add the milk and peanut butter and mix until incorporated, about 30 seconds. Then add the remaining flour and mix until just combined.

6. Remove the dough from the bowl, press it into a flat mound, and wrap it in plastic wrap. Let it chill in the refrigerator for at least 1 hour or up to 3 days.

7. While the dough is chilling, preheat the oven to 350°F. Line two sheet pans with parchment paper or spray lightly with nonstick cooking spray.

8. Remove the chilled dough from the refrigerator and scoop or roll it into balls about 1 tablespoon in size. Place the balls of dough about 1 inch apart on the prepared pans. Using your thumb or the back of a teaspoon measure, gently press the center of each dough ball to make an indentation in the top of each cookie.

9. Chill the cookie dough on the sheets in the refrigerator for about 10 minutes.

10. Bake for 12 to 15 minutes, rotating the pans once halfway through, until the edges of the cookies are golden brown. Remove the cookies from the oven, let them cool slightly on the pans, then transfer them to a wire rack to cool to room temperature.

11. While the cookies are cooling, prepare the ganache filling. Combine the milk chocolate chips, corn syrup, vanilla, and heavy cream in a mixing bowl and heat over a double boiler. Stir constantly with a rubber spatula or wooden spoon until the chocolate is fully melted and the ingredients have completely combined.

12. Once the chocolate mixture is smooth, take the bowl off the heat and add the peanut butter, stirring vigorously until combined.

13. Spoon the ganache filling into the indentations on each of the cookies. Let the ganache set at room temperature for 20 minutes.

14. Serve the cooled cookies immediately, or keep them in an airtight container at room temperature for up to 1 week.

POLISH YOUR LOOK Instead of using ganache, substitute ½ teaspoon of raspberry jam per cookie and fill the thumbprint of each cookie prior to baking. Bake as directed.

Linzer Thumbprints

MAKES ABOUT 3 DOZEN COOKIES

A slight twist on the classic linzer cookie, this thumbprint version is easier to prepare because it doesn't require rolling out dough. Hazelnuts are the nut traditionally used for this recipe, but almonds or pecans can also easily be substituted. When shopping for hazelnuts, be aware that "filbert" is another name for the nut and certain brands label them as such.

1	cup roasted hazelnuts
¾	cup plus 1 tablespoon sugar
1½	cups all-purpose flour
½	teaspoon baking powder
½	teaspoon salt
1½	teaspoons ground cinnamon
8	tablespoons (1 stick) chilled unsalted butter, cut into small pieces
1	large egg
1	tablespoon pure vanilla extract
1	cup raspberry jam (or any other favorite jam)

1. Using a food processor, grind the hazelnuts with 1 tablespoon sugar to a fine texture.

2. Combine the ground hazelnuts, flour, baking powder, salt, and cinnamon in a mixing bowl and gently whisk until all the ingredients are incorporated and there are no visible lumps in the flour.

3. Beat ¾ cup sugar and the butter in the bowl of a standing mixer fitted with a paddle attachment on medium-high speed until they form a coarse mixture, about 1 minute. (This recipe is different from other recipes using the creaming method because small chunks of butter will help give the dough a flaky texture. Just make sure that the butter pieces are no larger than the size of a pea.)

4. Mix the egg and vanilla with a fork in a small bowl. Add to the butter mixture and mix on medium-high speed until the ingredients are thoroughly combined, about 1 minute.

5. Add approximately half the flour and hazelnut mixture and mix on low speed just until the flour is incorporated, about 30 seconds. Scrape down the sides and bottom of the bowl to make sure that the flour is incorporated. Add the remaining flour and mix until just combined, about 15 seconds.

6. Remove the dough from the bowl. The dough will be somewhat dry, so press it firmly together onto a piece of plastic wrap. Wrap the dough with the plastic wrap, and let it chill in the refrigerator for at least 30 minutes or up to 3 days.

7. While the dough is chilling, preheat the oven to 350°F. Line two sheet pans with parchment paper or spray lightly with nonstick cooking spray.

8. Remove the chilled dough from the refrigerator and scoop or roll it into balls about 1 tablespoon in size. Place the balls of dough about 1 inch apart on the prepared sheet pans.

9. Using your thumb or the back of a teaspoon measure, gently make a depression in the top of each cookie. Spoon about ½ teaspoon jam into the depression of each cookie.

10. Bake for 18 to 20 minutes, rotating the pans once halfway through, until the cookie has darkened and become firm. Remove the cookies from the oven, let them cool slightly on the pans, then transfer them to a wire rack to cool to room temperature.

11. Serve the cooled cookies immediately, or keep them in an airtight container at room temperature for up to 4 days.

POLISH YOUR LOOK Bake the cookies without the jam and use half the hazelnut variation on the Basic Dark Chocolate Ganache recipe from Rich Chocolate Ganache Cake (page 111) to fill the thumbprints after they have cooled.

Chocolate Amaretto Thumbprints

MAKES ABOUT 3 DOZEN COOKIES

With its rich dark chocolate flavor and smooth, glossy ganache filling, this cookie easily transcends the basic cookie plate to more formal occasions. A dark chocolate amaretto ganache fills the center, but this recipe can also be made with espresso in the cookie and ganache, instead of amaretto, or you can try it with other liqueurs or flavorings.

Please note that the addition of the liqueur or espresso to this dough makes it much softer than the other thumbprint varieties, so the recipe requires a couple additional steps in order for the thumbprints to hold their shape.

1¼ **cups all-purpose flour**
½ **cup unsweetened cocoa powder**
2 **teaspoons baking powder**
8 **tablespoons (1 stick) unsalted butter, at room temperature**
¾ **cup sugar**
1 **large egg, at room temperature**
¼ **cup amaretto liqueur**

FOR THE FILLING

1 **cup (about 6 ounces) finely chopped dark chocolate**
¼ **cup heavy cream**
1 **tablespoon amaretto liqueur**

Sliced almonds, for garnish

1. Sift the flour, cocoa powder, and baking powder into a mixing bowl and set aside.

2. Beat the butter in the bowl of a standing mixer fitted with a paddle attachment at high speed until it is light and fluffy, about 3 minutes.

3. Add the sugar and mix on medium-high speed until smooth, about 1 minute. Scrape down the sides and bottom of the bowl with a rubber spatula halfway through mixing to ensure that the butter and sugar are well mixed.

4. Add the egg and mix until combined. Again, scrape down the sides and bottom of the bowl to make sure that the ingredients are incorporated.

5. Add approximately half the flour mixture and mix on low speed just until the flour is incorporated, about 30 seconds. Add the amaretto and then the remaining flour, mixing after each addition until just combined. Scrape down the sides and bottom of the bowl to ensure the flour is fully incorporated.

6. Remove the dough from the bowl and wrap it in plastic wrap. Let it chill in the refrigerator for at least 1 hour or up to 3 days.

7. While the dough is chilling, preheat the oven to 350°F. Line two sheet pans with parchment paper or spray lightly with nonstick cooking spray.

8. Remove the chilled dough from the refrigerator and scoop or roll it into balls about 1 tablespoon in size. Place the balls of dough about 1 inch apart on the prepared pans. Using your thumb or the back of a teaspoon measure, make a deep depression in each cookie (more than halfway down through the dough).

9. Place the sheet pans in the freezer for 15 minutes (this will help the cookies maintain their thumbprint shape while baking).

10. Bake for 12 to 15 minutes, rotating the pans once halfway through. The dough will spread a little, causing the depressions to lose their shape somewhat. When the cookies are firm around the edges and just a little soft in the center, remove them from the oven. Immediately use a teaspoon measure to reinforce the thumbprint depressions and let the cookies cool to room temperature on the pans.

11. While the cookies are baking and cooling, prepare the ganache filling. Combine the chocolate, heavy cream, and amaretto in a mixing bowl and heat over a double boiler. Stir constantly with a rubber spatula or wooden spoon until the chocolate is fully melted and the ingredients have completely combined. Set it aside to cool slightly, about 10 minutes.

12. When the ganache is cool enough that it is no longer runny, spoon it into the depressions of each cookie and top immediately with a sliced almond. Let the ganache set at room temperature for about 30 minutes.

13. Serve the cooled cookies immediately, or keep them in an airtight container at room temperature for up to 4 days.

Vanilla Cookies

THE CRISP OXFORD SHIRT

* **VANILLA COOKIE DOUGH**

* **Decorated Sugar Cookies**

* **Strawberry "Shortcakes"**

* **Royal Icing Cookies**

Cut-out Vanilla Cookies are clean and classic, making them the crisp oxford shirt of desserts. And, like an oxford shirt, they serve as a wonderful canvas for accessorizing.

The simplicity of this cookie makes it a good one to use for all sorts of purposes. Here we make it into Decorated Sugar Cookies, Strawberry "Shortcakes" (a great dessert canapé), and Royal Icing Cookies. The sugar cookies and Royal Icing Cookies are particularly fun to make with kids and are festive for holidays, birthdays, and other special events. All the recipes in this chapter can also be made with the Chocolate Cookie Dough (page 54) in the following chapter.

Vanilla Cookie Dough

MAKES 1 TO 4 DOZEN COOKIES (DEPENDING ON THE SIZE OF THE COOKIE CUTTERS)

This is one of the best cookie doughs to keep on hand in your freezer, especially if you have kids. Whether you are in need of a rainy day activity or a last-minute gift, pulling this dough out of the refrigerator or freezer, prerolled, gives you a solution at your fingertips. The only effort you will need to make depends on how you choose to decorate the cookies.

Because this is such a simple cookie, imperfections in the dough will be hard to hide. For that reason, it is especially important to beat the butter and brown sugar until they are completely smooth. Any lumps of either ingredient will cause noticeable imperfections in the baked cookie and make the cookie more difficult to decorate.

2¼ **cups all-purpose flour**
1 **teaspoon baking powder**
½ **teaspoon salt**
16 **tablespoons (2 sticks) unsalted butter, at room temperature**
¾ **cup packed light brown sugar**
1 **large egg, at room temperature**
1 **teaspoon pure vanilla extract**

1. Sift the flour, baking powder, and salt into a mixing bowl and set aside.

2. Beat the butter in the bowl of a standing mixer fitted with a paddle attachment at high speed until it is light and fluffy, about 3 minutes.

3. Add the brown sugar, crumbling it with your hands as you add it to get rid of any lumps. Mix on medium-high speed until smooth, about 1 minute. Scrape down the sides and bottom of the bowl with a rubber spatula halfway through mixing to ensure that the butter and sugar are well mixed.

4. Add the egg and vanilla and mix until combined. Again, scrape down the sides and bottom of the bowl to make sure that the ingredients are incorporated.

5. Add approximately half the flour mixture and mix on low speed just until the flour is incorporated, about 30 seconds. Repeat with the remaining flour. Scrape down the sides and bottom of the bowl to ensure the flour is fully incorporated.

6. Empty the dough onto a floured surface and gently push it together. Divide the dough in half and form each half into a flat disk 1 to 2 inches thick. Wrap each disk in plastic wrap and let it chill in the refrigerator for at least 1 hour or up to 3 days.

7. Once the dough has chilled, it can be rolled and used as directed (see Rolling Dough, page 10), or frozen in sheets (wrapped tightly on a sheet pan or piece of cardboard with plastic wrap) until needed or up to 2 months.

8. Cut and bake rolled dough as directed.

FASHION EMERGENCY Molasses is what makes brown sugar brown, but when it is exposed to air, it can lose its moisture and harden the sugar. To mitigate against this problem, try transferring leftover brown sugar from the box into a resealable plastic freezer bag and then storing the bag inside an airtight container. If your brown sugar hardens, you can soften it by microwaving it on high for 30 seconds, then crumble it with your hands and use it immediately. If the sugar is still hard or chunky after microwaving, discard it.

Decorated Sugar Cookies

MAKES 1 TO 3 DOZEN COOKIES (DEPENDING ON THE SIZE OF THE COOKIE CUTTERS)

Sprinkled sugar cookies are the easiest way to make a festive, special cookie in a variety of fun shapes. Making them is an easy activity to involve your kids in (especially younger ones). The cookies are a delicious, personalized gift for grandparents, teachers, or friends. You can stick with one shape of cookie cutter and one color of sprinkles, or you can mix and match for endless variations of this tasty treat.

> 1 **recipe Vanilla Cookie Dough (page 41)**
> ½ **cup egg whites (about 4 large eggs)**
> **Sanding sugar or sprinkles in assorted colors**

1. Preheat the oven to 350°F. Line two sheet pans with parchment paper or spray lightly with nonstick cooking spray.

2. Remove one disk of dough from the refrigerator and let it sit at room temperature for about 15 minutes. (The dough should be soft enough to roll without cracking, but not yet sticky.)

3. Place the dough on a piece of parchment paper or on a lightly floured flat surface. Lightly flour the top of the disk and begin rolling the dough (see Rolling Dough, page 10). Lift and rotate the dough between each roll to prevent it from sticking. Repeat the process until the dough is about ¼ inch thick (plus or minus about ⅛ inch; thicker for larger cookies, thinner for smaller ones).

4. Use your cookie cutters to cut out dough and place the shapes about 1 inch apart on the prepared pans. If the dough begins to stick to the cookie cutters, clean off any excess dough from the cutter and dip the edges of the cutter in flour. Repeat until the sheet pans are full. (The remaining dough can be kept in the refrigerator until it's ready to be used or baked. Rolled and/or cut dough can also be wrapped tightly and frozen.) Scraps of dough can be pushed together and rerolled twice. If the dough is rolled too many times, the flour will become overworked, and that will affect the texture of the cookies.

5. If the dough becomes soft in the rolling and cutting process, put the filled sheet pans in the refrigerator for 10 minutes, or until the cookies are firm again, before baking. Otherwise the cookies will lose their shape in the oven.

6. Lightly brush each cookie with some of the egg whites. (The cookies should look shiny, but have no visible buildup of egg whites.) Sprinkle the cookies with assorted sugar sprinkles.

7. Bake for 12 to 15 minutes (cooking time may vary, depending on the size of the cookies), rotating the pans once halfway through, until the edges of the cookies are golden brown. Remove the cookies from the oven, let them cool slightly on the pans, and transfer them to a wire rack to cool to room temperature. Repeat with the remaining dough, including the second disk.

8. Serve the cooled cookies immediately, or keep them in an airtight container for up to 1 week.

FASHION EMERGENCY Once you have rolled your dough three times, you can reserve your dough scraps for future use. In fact, some recipes in this book call for cookie crumbs from the Vanilla Cookie Dough (page 41), Chocolate Cookie Dough (page 54), and Graham Cracker Dough (page 86). Bake the dough scraps on a parchment-lined sheet pan at 350°F. Depending on the thickness of the scraps, they should be baked for 12 to 18 minutes. When they are done, they should be slightly darker and crispier than cookies baked from the same dough. After they have cooled to room temperature, the cookie scraps can be coarsely chopped (for ice cream toppings) or finely ground in a food processor (for cake toppings). They can be kept in an airtight container at room temperature for up to 2 weeks or frozen for up to 2 months.

Strawberry "Shortcakes"

MAKES ABOUT 4 DOZEN COOKIES

This is one of my favorite recipes for summer entertaining, and it works well for both casual and more formal events. These desserts can be set out on a tray at a backyard barbecue or passed with champagne at a swankier affair. The cookies are baked in a mini muffin pan in order to give them the shape of a small tartlet crust. Topping them with fresh whipped cream and macerated strawberries (strawberries that have been softened by soaking them in liquid) makes them a more unique option than traditional cookies, but they require minimal extra effort. Balsamic vinegar is a classic pairing with strawberries because the particularly sweet vinegar balances the sweet-tart flavor in the berries and brings out a more intense berry flavor.

> 1 **recipe Vanilla Cookie Dough (page 41)**
> 1 **pint fresh strawberries, stemmed and cut to a small dice**
> ¼ **cup plus 1 tablespoon sugar**
> 1 **tablespoon balsamic vinegar**
> 1 **pint heavy cream**

1. Preheat the oven to 350°F. Lightly spray a mini muffin pan with nonstick cooking spray and set aside.

2. Remove one disk of dough from the refrigerator and let it sit at room temperature until it is soft enough to roll without cracking, but not yet sticky.

3. Place the dough on a piece of parchment paper or on a lightly floured flat surface. Lightly flour the top of the disk and begin rolling the dough (see Rolling Dough, page 10). Lift and rotate the dough between each roll to prevent it from sticking. Repeat the process until the dough is about ⅛ inch thick.

4. Using a 1½- to 2-inch round cookie cutter, cut out rounds and press them gently into the bottom of each mini muffin cup, so that the bottom of each muffin cup is covered and some dough curls up the sides slightly. If the dough begins to stick to the cookie

cutter, clean off any excess dough from the cookie cutter and dip the edges of the cutter in flour. Repeat this process until the pan is full. (The remaining dough can be kept in the refrigerator until it's ready to be used or baked.)

5. Bake for 12 to 15 minutes, rotating the pan once halfway through, until the edges of the cookies are golden brown. Remove the cookie shells from the oven, let them cool slightly, then transfer them to a wire rack to cool to room temperature. Repeat, as desired, until all the dough is cut and baked, including the second disk, rerolling the dough as necessary, up to two more times. (Baked cookie shells can be kept in an airtight container at room temperature for up to 1 week.)

6. While the cookie shells are baking and cooling, put the diced strawberries in a mixing bowl. Sprinkle them with 1 tablespoon sugar and the vinegar and toss lightly to coat. Cover the bowl with plastic wrap and set it aside in the refrigerator for at least 30 minutes or overnight.

7. Whip the heavy cream in the bowl of a standing mixer fitted with a whisk attachment on medium-high speed. When the cream starts to thicken, and with the mixer running, slowly pour ¼ cup sugar into the cream. Continue to whip until the cream holds medium-firm peaks (it should be easy to spoon onto the cookies without losing its shape).

8. The whipped cream can be set aside in the refrigerator until ready to serve, or for up to 4 hours. Once you are ready to assemble the cookies, spoon or pipe about 1 teaspoon whipped cream onto each cookie and then top each with diced strawberries to fit. Serve immediately.

POLISH YOUR LOOK For weddings, wedding showers, or anniversary celebrations, turn the strawberries into a heart shape. When trimming the stems, carve a slight V shape into the top of the strawberry. Then, instead of dicing the strawberries, slice them about ⅛ inch thick perpendicular to the V cut. Macerate the strawberries as directed, then lay 1 slice on top of each whipped cream–topped cookie. (See photograph on page 46.)

Royal Icing Cookies

MAKES 1 TO 3 DOZEN COOKIES (DEPENDING ON THE SIZE OF THE COOKIE CUTTERS)

Royal icing is a sugar-and-egg-white-based frosting that fully hardens, making it a favorite icing for cookie decorating. Its pure white color also makes it easy to mix vibrant colors. Because the eggs aren't cooked, this recipe calls for pasteurized egg whites, which can be found in most grocery stores, but separated egg whites may be used as well. Alternatively, many specialty cake supply stores sell meringue powder or royal icing powder (see Resources, page 190) to which you need only add water (and sometimes confectioners' sugar) to mix it.

Frosting cookies with royal icing is somewhat difficult and takes practice to do really well, but once you've mastered it, it will take your holiday and special events cookies to a whole new level (see For Royal Icing Cookies, page 12).

1 **recipe Vanilla Cookie Dough (page 41)**
5 **ounces (⅝ cup) pasteurized egg whites or separated egg whites**
2 **pounds confectioners' sugar**
Food coloring in assorted colors

1. Preheat the oven to 350°F. Line two sheet pans with parchment paper or spray lightly with nonstick cooking spray.

2. Remove one disk of dough from the refrigerator and let it sit at room temperature for about 15 minutes. (The dough should be soft enough to roll without cracking, but not yet sticky.)

3. Place the dough on a piece of parchment paper or on a lightly floured flat surface. Lightly flour the top of the disk, and begin rolling the dough (see Rolling Dough, page 10). Lift and rotate the dough between each roll to prevent it from sticking. Repeat the process until the dough is approximately ¼ inch thick (plus or minus about ⅛ inch; thicker for larger cookies, thinner for smaller).

4. Use your cookie cutters to cut out dough and place the shapes about 1 inch apart on the prepared pans. If the dough begins to stick to the cookie cutters, clean off any excess dough

from the cutter and dip the edges of the cutter in flour. Repeat until the sheet pans are full. (The remaining dough can be kept in the refrigerator until it's ready to be used or baked. Rolled and/or cut dough can also be wrapped tightly and frozen.) Scraps of dough can be pushed together and rerolled twice.

5. If the dough becomes soft in the rolling and cutting process, put the filled sheet pans in the refrigerator for 10 minutes, or until the cookies are firm again, before baking. Otherwise the cookies will lose their shape in the oven.

6. Bake for 12 to 15 minutes (cooking time may vary, depending on the size of the cookies), rotating the pans once halfway through, until the edges of the cookies are golden brown. Remove the cookies from the oven, let them cool slightly on the pans, then transfer to a wire rack to cool to room temperature. Repeat with the remaining dough, including the second disk.

7. While the cookies are cooling, beat the egg whites in the bowl of a standing mixer fitted with the paddle attachment on medium-high speed until foamy, about 1 minute.

8. Add the confectioners' sugar and mix on low speed until combined, about 1 minute or until the paddle can be dipped in and out of the icing and a peak forms that holds its shape without falling back into the bowl.

9. Divide the icing in half, setting aside one half in a bowl covered with plastic wrap touching the surface of the icing. This half will be used for your flood.

10. Take the half that's uncovered and divide it further into as many batches as the number of colors you need. Mix in the food coloring. Be sure to cover any icing with plastic wrap when it's not in use, because it dries out quickly.

11. Fill a pastry bag fitted with a coupler and a small round tip with the stiff icing, one color at a time. (Be careful not to fill it with more than ½ to ¾ cup icing—more and it will be harder for you to control.) Use an offset spatula to push the icing toward the tip to avoid getting any air bubbles in the bag.

12. Pipe outlines along the edges of all the cookies, then set aside to dry (see Filling a Pastry Bag and Piping, page 11). Reserve any excess stiff icing.

13. Take the second half of the icing and add water, ½ teaspoon at a time, mixing thoroughly after each addition, until it is the consistency of thick paint. (When you run an

offset spatula through it, you should be able to make "ribbons" of icing that gradually absorb back into the mixture. If the ribbons absorb right away, add more confectioners' sugar, 1 tablespoon at a time, until you reach the desired flood consistency.)

14. Divide the flood icing into batches according to the number of colors desired and mix in the food coloring. Bear in mind that food coloring will thin the icing, so for deeper colors, start with a thicker flood. Again, be sure to cover any icing that is not in use with plastic wrap.

15. One color at a time, fill a squeeze bottle with the flood icing. (You can also use a pastry bag and tip, but squeeze bottles can be less messy.) Squeeze the icing onto the outlined cookies, as if you were coloring them in with a marker. The icing will spread to fill in most of the empty spaces. Use a toothpick or skewer to gently "pull" the icing into any open spaces so that no cookie is showing inside the outline. Repeat with other cookies and icing colors.

16. Once the cookies are flooded, let them dry, uncovered, overnight. If desired, finish them by piping words, monograms, or other details with the remaining stiff icing. For an added touch, before the stiff icing dries, take the cookie and place it facedown on a plate of sprinkles or sanding sugar, gently pressing the cookie so that the sprinkles adhere to the added words or other details. Let the icing dry before packaging or serving, about 1 hour.

17. The cookies can be kept in an airtight container for up to 1 week.

POLISH YOUR LOOK Royal icing can be mixed into an array of vivid colors. As you mix colors, add the food coloring judiciously, about a drop at a time, until you achieve your desired shade. Primary colors can be mixed to create a rainbow of other shades, just as you would mix paints. If you accidentally go too dark, you can adjust the icing with tablespoons of confectioners' sugar and drops of water to bring the icing back to a paler shade. Keep in mind that freshly mixed royal icing has a fair amount of air incorporated into it, so the color of your icing will darken as it dries. Finally, if you are working with bright colors, be sure to allow ample time for them to dry (at least 12 hours) before layering the cookie with paler shades, because the brighter colors can bleed into the paler ones.

Chocolate Cookies

THE
TRENCH COAT
....

* **CHOCOLATE COOKIE DOUGH**
* **Chocolate Cookie Sticks with Fondue**
* **Sandwich Cookies**
* **Ice Cream Sandwiches**
* **Chocolate Mint Cookies**

This chocolate version of our Vanilla Cookie Dough is still very much a basic, but the use of chocolate, like a trench coat, adds a timeless elegance to these cookies and easily takes your recipes from day to night. Also like a tailored trench coat, this chocolate dough has a quiet sophistication. It is extremely rich and not too sweet, which makes it a good option to use to make favors for special events such as an engagement party, retirement party, or milestone birthday party, when you want something that's customizable but also feels mature (see Royal Icing Cookies, page 49). This chapter also outlines a number of other different ways in which these chocolate cookies can be used for dinner parties, snacks, gifts, and more.

Any of the recipes from the previous chapter can also be made with this dough.

Chocolate Cookie Dough

MAKES 1 TO 4 DOZEN COOKIES (DEPENDING ON THE SIZE OF THE COOKIE CUTTERS)

While the Vanilla Cookie Dough (page 41) is good to have on hand and frozen for activities with kids, the chocolate version is perfect to keep stored if you do a lot of entertaining, as the last-minute preparation is just as easy, but the rich chocolate flavor makes it more appropriate for special occasions. By varying the thickness and size of the cookies, you can make them into a dainty dessert or a substantial accompaniment for a bowl of ice cream or chocolate mousse.

    1¾ **cups all-purpose flour**
      1 **cup unsweetened cocoa powder**
        Pinch of salt
   12 **tablespoons (1½ sticks) unsalted butter, at room temperature**
      1 **cup sugar**
      1 **large egg, at room temperature**

1. Sift the flour, cocoa powder, and salt into a mixing bowl and set aside.

2. Beat the butter in the bowl of a standing mixer fitted with a paddle attachment at high speed until it is light and fluffy, about 3 minutes.

3. Add the sugar and mix on medium–high speed until smooth, about 1 minute. Scrape down the sides and bottom of the bowl with a rubber spatula halfway through mixing to ensure that the butter and sugar are well mixed.

4. Add the egg and mix until combined. Again, scrape down the sides and bottom of the bowl to make sure that the ingredients are incorporated.

5. Add approximately half the flour-cocoa mixture and mix on low speed just until the flour is incorporated, about 30 seconds. Repeat with the remaining flour. Scrape down the sides and bottom of the bowl to ensure the flour is fully incorporated.

6. Empty the dough onto a lightly floured surface and gently push it together. Divide the dough in half and form each half into a flat disk 1 to 2 inches thick. Wrap each disk in plastic wrap and let it chill in the refrigerator for at least 1 hour or up to 3 days.

7. Once the dough has chilled, it can be rolled and used as directed (see Rolling Dough, page 10), or frozen in sheets (wrapped tightly with plastic wrap on a sheet pan or piece of cardboard) until needed or for up to 2 months.

8. Cut and bake rolled dough as directed.

Chocolate Cookie Sticks with Fondue

MAKES ENOUGH FOR 6 TO 8 PEOPLE

This fondue recipe is more of an accessory to than variation on the Chocolate Cookie Dough, but it makes a fun and unique addition to many desserts, especially chocolate cookies. Served with the cookies and a variety of fresh fruits, this chocolate fondue can make a conversation-starting dessert "station" for cocktail parties or a romantic treat after a dinner for two. This accessory also goes well as a sauce for ice cream or poured over a slice of Rich Chocolate Ganache Cake (page 111).

½ **recipe Chocolate Cookie Dough (page 54)**

FOR THE FONDUE

3 **cups (about 1 pound) bittersweet chocolate, chopped**
3 **tablespoons heavy cream**
3 **tablespoons light corn syrup**
3 **tablespoons kirsch or other liqueur (optional)**

Assorted fruits, such as strawberries, sliced apples, sliced bananas, for serving

1. Preheat the oven to 350°F. Line two sheet pans with parchment paper, or spray lightly with nonstick cooking spray.

2. Remove one disk of dough from the refrigerator and let it sit at room temperature for about 15 minutes. (The dough should be soft enough to roll without cracking, but not yet sticky.)

3. Place the dough on a piece of parchment paper or on a lightly floured flat surface. Lightly flour the top of the disk and begin rolling the dough (see Rolling Dough, page 10). Lift and rotate the dough between each roll to prevent it from sticking. Repeat the process until the dough is about ¼ inch thick.

4. Using a paring knife, slice the dough into rectangular sticks (approximately 4 inches by ½ inch) and place them about ½ inch apart on the prepared pans.

5. Bake for 10 to 12 minutes, rotating the pan once halfway through, until the edges of the cookies are firm. Remove the cookies from the oven, let them cool slightly on the pan, then transfer them to a wire rack to cool to room temperature. (The cookie sticks can be kept in an airtight container for up to 1 week.)

6. To make the fondue: Combine the bittersweet chocolate, heavy cream, corn syrup, and kirsch in a mixing bowl and heat over a double boiler. Stir constantly with a rubber spatula or wooden spoon until the chocolate is fully melted and all the ingredients have combined.

7. At this point, the fondue can be kept in an airtight container at room temperature for up to 4 hours or in the refrigerator for up to 1 week. Reheat it over a double boiler to bring it back to a liquid form before using.

8. When you are ready to serve it, transfer the fondue to a fondue pot and accompany it with the cookie sticks and assorted slices of fruit.

Sandwich Cookies

MAKES 2 TO 3 DOZEN COOKIES

These Sandwich Cookies are one of our signature items at Tribeca Treats. They are like homemade Oreos, but the fresh-baked cookies and the buttercream filling make them a richer, more delectable version. These cookies are also delicious when made with the Vanilla Cookie Dough (page 41) or Graham Cracker Dough (page 86) and using a variety of fillings, including vanilla buttercream, chocolate ganache, cinnamon cream cheese, marshmallow icing, peanut butter icing, and caramel. Use your imagination to mix and match and create a wide variety of cookies.

1 recipe Chocolate Cookie Dough (page 54)
¼ recipe Vanilla Icing (page 136)

1. Preheat the oven to 350°F. Line two sheet pans with parchment paper or spray lightly with nonstick cooking spray.

2. Remove one disk of dough from the refrigerator and let it sit at room temperature for about 15 minutes. (The dough should be soft enough to roll without cracking, but not yet sticky.)

3. Place the dough on a piece of parchment paper or on a lightly floured flat surface. Lightly flour the top of the disk and begin rolling the dough (see Rolling Dough, page 10). Lift and rotate the dough between each roll to prevent it from sticking. Repeat the process until the dough is between ⅛ and ¼ inch thick.

4. Using a 1½-inch round cookie cutter, cut out cookies and place them about ½ inch apart on the prepared pans. Repeat until the pans are full. (The remaining dough can be kept in the refrigerator until ready to be used.)

5. Bake for 12 to 15 minutes, rotating the pans once halfway through, until the edges of the cookies are firm. Remove the cookies from the oven, let them cool slightly on the pans, then transfer them to a wire rack to cool to room temperature.

6. While the cookies are cooling, prepare the Vanilla Icing if you have not already done so. Set it aside.

7. On a separate sheet pan or work surface, place half the cookies bottom side up. Fill a pastry bag with icing (no tip is necessary) and pipe about 1 teaspoon icing onto each cookie bottom.

8. Take the remaining cookies and gently press one on top of each iced cookie, bottom side down, to form a sandwich. Allow the cookies to set at room temperature for about 30 minutes before serving or packaging.

9. The cookies can be stored in an airtight container at room temperature for up to 1 week.

Ice Cream Sandwiches

MAKES ABOUT 1 DOZEN SANDWICHES

Although you can use any of your favorite ice creams with the Chocolate, Vanilla, or Graham Cracker Cookie doughs, the Chocolate Cookie Dough pairs best with the widest variety of ice cream flavors.

1 recipe Chocolate Cookie Dough (page 54)
2 pints vanilla ice cream
1 cup chocolate or rainbow sprinkles, or mini semisweet chocolate chips

1. Preheat the oven to 350°F. Line two sheet pans with parchment paper or spray lightly with nonstick cooking spray.

2. Remove one disk of dough from the refrigerator and let it sit at room temperature for about 15 minutes. (The dough should be soft enough to roll without cracking, but not yet sticky.)

3. Place the dough on a piece of parchment paper or on a lightly floured flat surface. Lightly flour the top of the disk and begin rolling the dough (see Rolling Dough, page 10). Lift and rotate the dough between each roll to prevent it from sticking. Repeat the process until the dough is a little less than ¼ inch thick.

4. Using a 3-inch round cookie cutter, cut out cookies and place them about ½ inch apart on the prepared pans. Repeat until the pans are full. (The remaining dough can be kept in the refrigerator until ready to be used.)

5. Bake for 12 to 15 minutes, rotating the pans once halfway through, until the edges of the cookies are firm. Remove the cookies from the oven, let them cool slightly on the pans, then transfer them to a wire rack to cool to room temperature.

6. While the cookies are baking and cooling, take 1 pint of ice cream out of the freezer and let it soften at room temperature for 5 to 10 minutes.

7. While the ice cream is softening, line the insides of 6 to 8 individual ramekins (about 2½ inches in diameter) with plastic wrap (or use a silicone mold with 2½- to 3-inch round cups).

8. Scoop the ice cream evenly into the ramekins and, using a small offset spatula, spread the ice cream flat inside each ramekin. Place the ramekins in the freezer and let them set for about 1 hour.

9. Once the ice cream in the ramekins has set, remove the molded ice cream disks from the ramekins, place them on a plate (still in their plastic wrappers or on a layer of parchment or waxed paper), and return them to the freezer while you repeat the molding process with the second pint of ice cream.

10. Once the second batch of ice cream has set, place half the cookies bottom side up on a sheet pan or work surface. Unwrap each portion of molded ice cream and place it on a cookie bottom. Take the remaining cookies and place one, bottom side down, on top of each ice cream disk. Gently press each pair of cookies together to adhere the ice cream to the cookies. Return the sandwiches to the freezer to set for about 10 minutes.

11. Place the sprinkles in a shallow bowl. Pour warm water into a small cup and set it aside.

12. Remove the ice cream sandwiches from the freezer. Working quickly, dip a small offset spatula into the warm water and run it lightly along the sides of the ice cream. Then roll the sandwich in the sprinkles, so that they adhere to the ice cream.

13. Repeat with all the ice cream sandwiches, then return them to the freezer to set (on a plate or sheet pan) for at least 1 hour or up to 1 month. (Wrap the sandwiches tightly with plastic wrap if you are freezing them for more than 12 hours.)

FASHION EMERGENCY For a faster, easier way to make the ice cream sandwiches, you can eliminate the steps for molding the ice cream and place a scoop of ice cream directly onto half the cookies bottom side up. Let the ice cream soften for about 1 minute, then take the remaining cookies and gently press the ice cream down to sandwich it. Let the ice cream sandwiches set in the freezer, as directed. Molding the ice cream gives you a cleaner, more polished-looking final product, but this process will save you time and effort.

Chocolate Mint Cookies

MAKES ABOUT 5 DOZEN COOKIES

The homemade version of the Girl Scouts' Thin Mints cookies. Need I say more?

1¾ **cups all-purpose flour**
1 **cup unsweetened cocoa powder**
   Pinch of salt
12 **tablespoons (1½ sticks) unsalted butter, at room temperature**
1 **cup sugar**
1 **large egg, at room temperature**
2 **teaspoons mint extract**
3 **cups (about 1 pound) finely chopped bittersweet chocolate**
1 **teaspoon vegetable oil (not necessary if tempering chocolate)**

1. Sift the flour, cocoa powder, and salt into a mixing bowl and set aside.

2. Beat the butter in the bowl of a standing mixer fitted with a paddle attachment at high speed until it is light and fluffy, about 3 minutes.

3. Add the sugar and mix on medium-high speed until smooth, about 1 minute. Scrape down the sides and bottom of the bowl with a rubber spatula halfway through mixing to ensure that the butter and sugar are well mixed.

4. Add the egg and mint extract and mix until combined. Again, scrape down the sides and bottom of the bowl to make sure that the ingredients are incorporated.

5. Add approximately half the flour-cocoa mixture and mix on low speed just until the mixture is incorporated, about 30 seconds. Repeat with the remaining flour-cocoa mixture. Scrape down the sides and bottom of the bowl to ensure the flour is fully incorporated.

6. Empty the dough onto a lightly floured surface and gently push it together. Divide the dough in half and form each half into a flat disk 1 to 2 inches thick. Wrap each disk in plastic wrap and let it chill in the refrigerator for at least 1 hour or up to 3 days.

7. While the dough is chilling, preheat the oven to 350°F. Line two sheet pans with parchment paper or spray lightly with nonstick cooking spray.

8. Remove one disk of dough from the refrigerator and let it sit at room temperature for about 15 minutes. (The dough should be soft enough to roll without cracking, but not yet sticky.)

9. Place the dough on a piece of parchment paper or on a lightly floured flat surface. Lightly flour the top of the disk and begin rolling the dough (see Rolling Dough, page 10). Lift and rotate the dough between each roll to prevent it from sticking. Repeat the process until the dough is ⅛ inch thick.

10. Using a 1½- to 2-inch round cookie cutter, cut out cookies and place them about ½ inch apart on the prepared pans. Repeat until the pans are full. (The remaining dough can be kept in the refrigerator until ready to be used.)

11. Bake for 10 to 12 minutes, rotating the pans once halfway through, until the edges of the cookies are firm. Remove the cookies from the oven, let them cool slightly on the pan, then transfer them to a wire rack to cool to room temperature.

12. While the cookies are cooling, begin tempering the chocolate (see Basic Tempered Chocolate, page 163), or heat the chocolate and oil over a double boiler. Stir constantly with a rubber spatula or wooden spoon until the chocolate has just melted. Remove the bowl from the heat and let the chocolate cool at room temperature for 5 minutes before using.

13. Line a sheet pan with parchment paper. Using an offset spatula or fork, dip each cookie into the chocolate so that it is fully immersed, and then scrape it against the lip of the bowl to remove any excess chocolate as you remove the cookie from the chocolate (see Dipping in Chocolate, page 17). Set each cookie on the sheet pan and gently tap the

tines of a fork against the top of the cookie, forming a pattern of parallel lines as texture in the melted chocolate. Allow the cookies to set at room temperature for about 45 minutes (or 20 minutes in the refrigerator).

14. Serve the cooled cookies immediately, or keep them in an airtight container at room temperature for up to 1 week.

Brownies

THE CASHMERE SWEATER
....

* **FUDGY BROWNIES**
* **Brownie Sundae Parfait**
* **Peanut Butter Brownies**
* **Mint Swirl Brownies**

What cashmere does for sweaters, this recipe does for brownies. Just as the lush fabric can make a comfortable item elegant, this dense, fudgy brownie has a low flour-to-sugar ratio, giving it a more intense chocolate flavor than its crumbly, cakey counterpart. The fudginess also helps keep it shelf-stable longer and makes it a great treat to keep frozen for later—just defrost and serve.

I recommend that you bake these brownies in a metal pan, as it will allow the heat to more thoroughly permeate the batter. If you don't have metal pans in the sizes called for in the recipes, you can use a glass baking dish—just add 5 to 10 minutes to the cooking time. A double batch of any of the recipes here will fit in a sheet pan.

Fudgy Brownies

MAKES 2 TO 3 DOZEN BROWNIES

At the risk of offending traditional pastry chefs, I'll admit that I'm actually a big fan of boxed brownie mixes. They're always easy to make, and since the brownie is such a basic dessert, there's often no need to get fancy. However, if you do have a little extra time, making them from scratch with good-quality bittersweet chocolate really elevates the flavor and texture, taking them from an after-school snack to a decadent dessert.

16 tablespoons (2 sticks) unsalted butter, at room temperature
1¼ cups semisweet chocolate chips or 8 ounces finely chopped bittersweet chocolate
4 large eggs, at room temperature
1 cup plus 1 tablespoon granulated sugar
1 cup plus 1 tablespoon packed dark brown sugar
1 tablespoon pure vanilla extract
Pinch of salt
¾ cup all-purpose flour

1. Preheat the oven to 350°F. Line a 9-inch square metal baking pan with parchment paper and spray lightly with nonstick cooking spray. (Please note: Unlike the cookie recipes where you can use either parchment paper or nonstick cooking spray, in this recipe the relative sugar content in the brownies requires both the parchment paper and cooking spray for cooking. Otherwise the brownies will stick to the pan.)

2. Heat the butter and chocolate in a bowl over a double boiler. Stir constantly with a rubber spatula or wooden spoon, until the butter and chocolate are fully melted and combined. Remove the bowl from the heat and cool to room temperature.

3. Whisk the eggs in a large mixing bowl. Add the granulated sugar, brown sugar, vanilla, and salt, and continue to whisk until they are all combined. Add the melted chocolate slowly and whisk until incorporated, about 1 minute.

4. Once the chocolate is incorporated, sift the flour into the bowl and gently stir with a rubber spatula until the flour is combined, about 1 minute.

5. Pour the brownie batter into the prepared pan. Bake for 45 to 50 minutes, rotating the pan once halfway through. Before removing the pan from the oven, gently shake it—if the middle of the brownies remains still, they are done. Run a knife along the sides of the pan and allow the brownies to cool in the pan to room temperature, about 1 hour.

6. Once cooled, the brownies can be sliced and served immediately, kept in an airtight container at room temperature for up to 1 week, or wrapped tightly and frozen for up to 8 weeks.

FASHION EMERGENCY For best results in trimming and cutting brownies, after the brownies have come to room temperature in the pan, place the pan in the refrigerator for at least 1 hour. Once the brownies have chilled, remove them from the pan, remove the parchment paper lining the bottom of the brownies, then flip them right side up onto a cutting board. Use a large chef's knife, with a damp hot towel nearby, to first trim the edges (about ½ inch) around all sides. Then score the brownies lightly with your knife to mark the grid by which you would like to cut them. Finally, in a smooth motion, drag the knife through the lines of the grid to cut the brownies into pieces. Be sure to use the damp towel to wipe the knife clean if it accumulates brownie crumbs between slices.

Brownie Sundae Parfait

MAKES 6 INDIVIDUAL DESSERTS

This is a great dessert to vary, according to your cravings and mood, with different flavors of ice cream and sauces. I love the uncomplicated taste of vanilla bean ice cream with brownies, but go for any of your favorite flavors. The Caramel Sauce adds another dimension of flavor and color to the chocolate and vanilla, but many other traditional ice cream sauces will also work. I like to spoon a little of the sauce between the brownies and ice cream to prevent the brownie layer from tasting too dry. The sauce helps pack it together with a nice gooey consistency, so that it's not too much of a textural contrast from the ice cream.

> 3 **cups leftover Fudgy Brownies (page 67), roughly chopped into small (about ½ inch) pieces**
> 1 **cup Caramel Sauce (page 186) or store-bought sauce**
> 1 **pint vanilla ice cream**
> 2 **cups whipped cream**

1. Place ¼ cup brownies in the bottom of each of 6 parfait glasses.

2. Drizzle about 1 tablespoon of the Caramel Sauce into each glass, then scoop half the pint of ice cream evenly among the glasses. Drizzle with another tablespoon of sauce.

3. Repeat with one more layer of brownies, caramel, ice cream, and caramel sauce. Top each parfait with a scoop of whipped cream and serve immediately.

POLISH YOUR LOOK Try the parfait with Peanut Butter Brownies (page 72), chocolate or banana ice cream, and Caramel Sauce. Or try the Mint Swirl Brownies (page 74) with mint ice cream and chocolate fondue (see Chocolate Cookie Sticks with Fondue, page 56).

Peanut Butter Brownies

MAKES 2 TO 3 DOZEN BROWNIES

Baking sweet peanut butter icing into the top layer of the brownies brings more depth to both flavors and is another way to highlight the ever-popular peanut butter and chocolate combination. These rich treats are a resounding hit at tailgate parties and make a comforting get-well gift for a peanut butter–loving friend.

16	tablespoons (2 sticks) unsalted butter, at room temperature
1¼	cups semisweet chocolate chips or 8 ounces finely chopped bittersweet chocolate
4	large eggs, at room temperature
1	cup plus 1 tablespoon granulated sugar
1	cup plus 1 tablespoon packed dark brown sugar
1	tablespoon pure vanilla extract
	Pinch of salt
¾	cup all-purpose flour
¾	cup creamy peanut butter
¼	cup confectioners' sugar
¼	cup heavy cream

1. Preheat the oven to 350°F. Line a 9 x 13-inch metal baking pan with parchment paper and spray lightly with nonstick cooking spray. (Please note: Unlike the cookie recipes where you can use either parchment paper or nonstick cooking spray, in this recipe the relative sugar content in the brownies requires both the parchment paper and cooking spray for cooking. Otherwise the brownies will stick to the pan.)

2. Heat the butter and chocolate in a bowl over a double boiler. Stir constantly with a rubber spatula or wooden spoon until the butter and chocolate are fully melted and combined. Remove the bowl from the heat and cool to room temperature.

3. Whisk the eggs in a large mixing bowl. Add the granulated sugar, brown sugar, vanilla, and salt, and continue to whisk until they are all combined. Add the melted chocolate slowly and whisk until incorporated, about 1 minute.

4. Once the chocolate is incorporated, sift the flour into the bowl and gently stir with a rubber spatula until the flour is combined, about 1 minute. Pour the brownie batter into the prepared pan and set aside.

5. Mix the peanut butter, confectioners' sugar, and heavy cream in a bowl and stir vigorously with a large fork to combine. Spoon dollops of the peanut butter mixture into the brownie batter, distributing it evenly. Run a knife through the pan to marbleize the peanut butter into the brownie batter.

6. Bake for 45 to 50 minutes, rotating the pan once halfway through. Before removing the brownies from the oven, gently shake the pan—if the middle of the brownies remains still, the brownies are done. Run a knife along the sides of the pan and allow the brownies to cool in the pan to room temperature, about 1 hour.

7. Once cooled, the brownies can be sliced and served immediately, kept in an airtight container at room temperature for up to 1 week, or wrapped tightly and frozen for up to 8 weeks.

Mint Swirl Brownies

MAKES 2 TO 3 DOZEN BROWNIES

The mint element of these brownies is incorporated differently from the way the peanut butter was in the previous recipe. Mint extract is added to the base brownie batter and then an additional mint cream layer is made, using a batter similar to cheesecake. The cream cheese layer requires the brownies to be cooked for longer at a lower temperature. The resulting dessert has a rich texture but a somewhat less intense chocolate flavor than the other brownie recipes. The sour tang of the cream cheese also tempers the sweetness of this treat.

FOR THE BROWNIE LAYER

- 16 tablespoons (2 sticks) unsalted butter, at room temperature
- 1¼ cups semisweet chocolate chips or 8 ounces finely chopped bittersweet chocolate
- 4 large eggs, at room temperature
- 1 cup plus 1 tablespoon granulated sugar
- 1 cup plus 1 tablespoon packed dark brown sugar
- 1 tablespoon mint extract
- Pinch of salt
- ¾ cup all-purpose flour

FOR THE MINT CREAM LAYER

- One 8-ounce package cream cheese
- ⅓ cup granulated sugar
- 1 tablespoon mint extract
- 1 large egg, at room temperature

1. Preheat the oven to 325°F. Line a 9 x 13-inch metal baking pan with parchment paper and spray lightly with nonstick cooking spray. (Please note: Unlike the cookie recipes where you can use either parchment paper or nonstick cooking spray, in this recipe the relative sugar content in the brownies requires both the parchment paper and cooking spray for cooking. Otherwise the brownies will stick to the pan.

2. Heat the butter and chocolate in a bowl over a double boiler. Stir constantly with a rubber spatula or wooden spoon until the butter and chocolate are fully melted and combined. Remove the bowl from the heat and cool to room temperature.

3. Whisk the eggs in a large mixing bowl. Add the granulated sugar, brown sugar, mint extract, and salt, and continue to whisk until they are all combined. Add the melted chocolate and whisk until incorporated, about 1 minute.

4. Once the chocolate is incorporated, sift the flour into the bowl and gently stir with a rubber spatula until the flour is combined, about 1 minute. Pour the brownie batter into the prepared pan and set aside.

5. For the mint cream layer, combine the cream cheese, granulated sugar, mint extract, and egg in a food processor or a mixer and blend for about 2 minutes. Pour the mint cream evenly over the brownie batter and run a knife or skewer through the pan to marbleize the batter.

6. Bake for 50 to 60 minutes, rotating the pan once halfway through. Before removing the brownies from the oven, gently shake the pan—if the middle of the brownies remains still, the brownies are done. Run a knife along the sides of the pan and allow the brownies to cool in the pan to room temperature, about 1 hour.

7. Once cooled, the brownies can be sliced and served immediately, kept in an airtight container at room temperature for up to 1 week, or wrapped tightly and frozen for up to 8 weeks.

Buttermilk Cookies

THE PEARL EARRINGS

·················

* **MINI BLACK AND WHITE COOKIES**
* **Lime-Glazed Tea Cookies**
* **Cinnamon-Glazed Tea Cookies**

Prim and ladylike, buttermilk cookies go with any occasion from brunch to evening. The cookie itself has a consistency somewhere between a cookie and a cake; the buttermilk helps soften the glutens in the flour to keep it from being too chewy. These cookies are not as buttery as some other varieties and their flavor is fairly delicate, so they depend on the icing to strengthen the flavor and keep them from drying out. The lime and cinnamon versions of these cookies demonstrate how you can take them in different flavor directions simply by adding a different zest, spice, or essence into the cookie and icing. Like a nice pair of pearl earrings, these buttermilk cookie recipes could have been passed down from your grandmother, but the way you style them makes them all yours.

Mini Black and White Cookies

MAKES ABOUT 3 DOZEN COOKIES

The black and white cookie is a New York institution. The version found in almost every corner deli is about three times the size of these, but this smaller one is popular for parties because it's more manageable to eat in a social setting. At Tribeca Treats customers frequently order them as favors for weddings or black-and-white color-schemed events.

Traditionally, the icing is applied to the bottom, or flat side, of the cookie. Doing so helps you create a neat delineation between your chocolate and white icings. Having the rounded side as the bottom also adds a topsy-turvy playfulness when plating them.

3 cups all-purpose flour

½ teaspoon baking soda

½ teaspoon salt

12 tablespoons (1½ sticks) unsalted butter, at room temperature

1½ cups sugar

2 large eggs, at room temperature

1 teaspoon pure vanilla extract

⅔ cup buttermilk

FOR THE GLAZES

1½ cups confectioners' sugar

¼ cup buttermilk

½ cup unsweetened cocoa powder

1. Preheat the oven to 350°F. Line two sheet pans with parchment paper or spray lightly with nonstick cooking spray.

2. Sift the flour, baking soda, and salt into a mixing bowl and set aside.

3. Beat the butter in the bowl of a standing mixer fitted with a paddle attachment at high speed until it is light and fluffy, about 3 minutes.

4. Add the sugar and continue to mix on medium-high speed until smooth, about 1 minute. Scrape down the sides and bottom of the bowl with a rubber spatula halfway through mixing to ensure that the butter and sugar are well mixed.

5. Add the eggs and mix until combined. Again, scrape down the sides and bottom of the bowl to make sure that the ingredients are incorporated.

6. Add approximately half the flour mixture and mix on low speed just until the mixture is incorporated, about 30 seconds. Add the vanilla and buttermilk and mix until combined, about 15 seconds.

7. Add the remaining flour and mix until combined, about 15 seconds. Remove the bowl from the mixer and scrape down the sides and bottom of the bowl with a rubber spatula to make sure that the flour is fully incorporated. Compared with other, drier cookie doughs, this dough has a more pasty consistency.

8. Using a small ice cream scoop or a tablespoon measure, scoop the cookie dough about 1 inch apart onto the prepared pans. Bake for 18 to 20 minutes, rotating the pans once halfway through, until the edges of the cookies are golden brown. Remove the cookies from the oven and let them cool on the pans to room temperature.

9. While the cookies are cooling, prepare the white glaze. Sift 1 cup confectioners' sugar into a small bowl. Add 2 tablespoons buttermilk and mix thoroughly with a fork.

10. Once the cookies are at room temperature, flip them over and, using a small offset spatula, spread the white glaze over one-half of the bottom of each cookie.

11. While the white glaze sets, sift ½ cup confectioners' sugar and ½ cup cocoa powder into another bowl and add 2 tablespoons buttermilk. Mix thoroughly with a fork. Using a small offset spatula, spread the chocolate glaze onto the other half of each cookie. Allow the cookies to set for 20 minutes.

12. Serve the set cookies immediately, or keep them in an airtight container at room temperature for up to 4 days.

Lime-Glazed Tea Cookies

MAKES ABOUT 3 DOZEN COOKIES

The lime version of the buttermilk cookie is a tart, refreshing treat—perfect for a summer day. You can also easily substitute lemon or orange for the lime; all are especially welcome at brunches or tea parties. This recipe directs you to spoon the icing over the tops of the cookies, but if you like the playfulness of the rounded bottoms from the Mini Black and White Cookies (page 77), you can flip them over and ice the bottoms using the same technique.

 3 **cups all-purpose flour**
 ½ **teaspoon baking soda**
 ½ **teaspoon salt**
 12 **tablespoons (1½ sticks) unsalted butter, at room temperature**
 1½ **cups sugar**
 2 **tablespoons freshly grated lime zest**
 2 **large eggs, at room temperature**
 2 **teaspoons fresh lime juice**
 ⅔ **cup buttermilk**

 FOR THE GLAZE
 2 **cups confectioners' sugar**
 2 **tablespoons fresh lime juice**
 2 **tablespoons buttermilk**

1. Preheat the oven to 350°F. Line two sheet pans with parchment paper or spray lightly with nonstick cooking spray.

2. Sift the flour, baking soda, and salt into a mixing bowl and set aside.

3. Beat the butter in the bowl of a standing mixer fitted with a paddle attachment at high speed until it is light and fluffy, about 3 minutes.

4. Add the sugar and lime zest and continue to mix on medium-high speed until smooth, about 1 minute. Scrape down the sides and bottom of the bowl with a rubber spatula halfway through mixing to ensure that the butter, sugar, and zest are well mixed.

5. Add the eggs and mix until combined. Again, scrape down the sides and bottom of the bowl to make sure that the ingredients are incorporated.

6. Add approximately half the flour mixture and mix on low speed just until the flour is incorporated, about 30 seconds. Add the lime juice and buttermilk and mix until combined, about 15 seconds.

7. Add the remaining flour and mix until combined, about 15 seconds. Remove the bowl from the mixer and scrape down the sides and bottom of the bowl with a rubber spatula to make sure that the flour is fully incorporated. Compared with other, drier cookie doughs, this dough has a more pasty consistency.

8. Using a small ice cream scoop or a tablespoon measure, scoop the cookie dough about ½ inch apart onto the prepared pans. Bake for 18 to 20 minutes, rotating the pans once halfway through, until the edges of the cookies are golden brown. Remove the cookies from the oven and let them cool on the pans to room temperature.

9. While the cookies are cooling, prepare the glaze. Sift the confectioners' sugar into a mixing bowl. Add the lime juice and buttermilk and mix with a fork until smooth.

10. Transfer the room-temperature cookies to a wire rack set over a sheet of parchment or waxed paper and spoon the glaze over them. Allow the glaze to set for 20 minutes.

11. Serve the cooled cookies immediately, or keep them in an airtight container at room temperature for up to 4 days.

Cinnamon-Glazed Tea Cookies

MAKES ABOUT 3 DOZEN COOKIES

This cinnamon-glazed cookie is French toast in cookie form—a breadlike texture with cinnamon-sweet flavor. You can add chopped candied pecans by sprinkling them onto the cookie after it's iced but while the icing is still wet. This recipe directs you to spoon the icing over the tops of the cookies, but if you like the playfulness of the rounded bottoms from the Mini Black and White Cookies (page 77), you can flip them over and ice the bottoms using the same technique.

3 **cups all-purpose flour**
½ **teaspoon baking soda**
1 **tablespoon ground cinnamon**
½ **teaspoon salt**
12 **tablespoons (1½ sticks) unsalted butter, at room temperature**
1½ **cups sugar**
2 **large eggs, at room temperature**
1 **teaspoon pure vanilla extract**
⅔ **cup buttermilk**

FOR THE GLAZE
2 **cups confectioners' sugar**
2 **tablespoons ground cinnamon**
¼ **cup buttermilk**

1. Preheat the oven to 350°F. Line two sheet pans with parchment paper or spray lightly with nonstick cooking spray.

2. Sift the flour, baking soda, cinnamon, and salt in a mixing bowl and set aside.

3. Beat the butter in the bowl of a standing mixer fitted with a paddle attachment at high speed until it is light and fluffy, about 3 minutes.

4. Add the sugar and continue to mix on medium-high speed until smooth, about 1 minute. Scrape down the sides and bottom of the bowl with a rubber spatula halfway through mixing to ensure that the butter and sugar are well mixed.

5. Add the eggs and mix until combined. Again, scrape down the sides and bottom of the bowl to make sure that the ingredients are combined.

6. Add approximately half the flour mixture and mix on low speed just until the flour is incorporated, about 30 seconds. Add the vanilla and buttermilk and mix until combined, about 15 seconds.

7. Add the remaining flour and mix until combined, about 15 seconds. Remove the bowl from the mixer and scrape down the sides and bottom of the bowl with a rubber spatula to make sure that the flour is fully incorporated. Compared with other, drier cookie doughs, this dough has a more pasty consistency.

8. Using a small ice cream scoop or a tablespoon measure, scoop the cookie dough about 1 inch apart onto the prepared pans. Bake for 18 to 20 minutes, rotating the pans once halfway through, until the edges of the cookies are golden brown. Remove the cookies from the oven and let them cool on the pans to room temperature.

9. While the cookies are cooling, prepare the glaze. Sift the confectioners' sugar and cinnamon into a mixing bowl. Add the buttermilk and mix with a fork until smooth.

10. Transfer the room-temperature cookies to a wire rack set over a sheet of parchment or waxed paper and spoon the glaze over them. Allow the glaze to set for 20 minutes.

11. Serve the cooled cookies immediately, or keep them in an airtight container at room temperature for up to 4 days.

Graham Crackers

THE PERFECT-FIT JEANS
....

* **GRAHAM CRACKER DOUGH**
* **Cinnamon Cream Cheese Sandwich Cookies**
* **S'mores Cookies**

The right pair of jeans makes you both look good and feel good, so too do these cookies. You look good when you whip out a plate of cookies and your friends can't believe you made your own graham crackers. You feel good when you enjoy the unaccessorized graham crackers as a snack and, with whole wheat flour and wheat germ, the crackers make for a more healthful alternative to the Fudgy Brownies you ate last week.

Homemade graham crackers are far more flavorful than the store-bought version; you can taste several elements, including the wheat, cinnamon, and honey, in each bite. These cookies are also softer than the store-bought variety. For a crispier version, bake them for two to four minutes longer than you do when using them for Sandwich or S'mores cookies.

Wheat germ adds texture to the cookies and also helps give them a toasty flavor. Commonly found near the flour in grocery stores, wheat germ is typically packaged in a jar, and, for best storage, the jar should be refrigerated after it's opened.

Graham Cracker Dough

MAKES ABOUT 2 DOZEN CRACKERS

These cookies are just as tasty eaten plain as they are in any of the variations in this chapter. Steps 6 through 12 of this recipe outline how to bake them on their own for a snack. If you are using the dough for another recipe in this chapter, stop at step 5.

½ **cup all-purpose flour**

½ **cup whole wheat flour**

¼ **cup untoasted wheat germ**

¼ **teaspoon salt**

½ **teaspoon baking soda**

½ **teaspoon ground cinnamon**

8 **tablespoons (1 stick) unsalted butter, at room temperature**

½ **cup packed light brown sugar**

2 **tablespoons honey**

**FOR THE COATING
(IF YOU ARE EATING THEM
ON THEIR OWN)**

2 **tablespoons granulated sugar**

2 **tablespoons ground cinnamon**

1. Put the all-purpose flour, wheat flour, wheat germ, salt, baking soda, and cinnamon in a mixing bowl and gently whisk until all the ingredients are incorporated and there are no visible lumps.

2. Beat the butter in the bowl of a standing mixer fitted with a paddle attachment at high speed until it is light and fluffy, about 3 minutes.

3. Add the brown sugar, crumbling it with your hands as you add it to remove any lumps, and mix on medium-high speed until smooth, about 1 minute. Add the honey and mix until combined. Scrape down the sides and bottom of the bowl using a rubber spatula halfway through mixing to ensure that the ingredients are combined.

4. Add approximately half the flour mixture and mix on low speed just until the flour is incorporated, about 30 seconds. Repeat with the remaining flour. Scrape down the sides and bottom of the bowl to ensure the flour is fully incorporated.

5. Empty the dough onto a lightly floured surface and gently push it together. Form it into a flat disk 1 to 2 inches thick. Wrap the dough in plastic wrap and let it chill in the refrigerator for at least 30 minutes or up to 4 days.

6. Once the dough has chilled, it can be rolled and used as directed (see Rolling Dough, page 10), or frozen in sheets (wrapped tightly with plastic wrap on a sheet pan or piece of cardboard) until needed or for up to 2 months.

7. If baking immediately, preheat the oven to 350°F. Line two sheet pans with parchment paper or spray lightly with nonstick cooking spray.

8. Place the dough on a piece of parchment paper or on a lightly floured flat surface. Lightly flour the top of the disk and begin rolling the dough. Lift and rotate the dough between each roll to prevent it from sticking. Repeat the process until the dough is between ⅛ and ¼ inch thick.

9. Using a paring knife, cut the dough into 2-inch squares and place them about ½ inch apart on the prepared pans.

10. To coat, combine the granulated sugar and cinnamon in a small bowl and toss lightly with a fork. Sprinkle the dough with the sugar mixture.

11. Bake for 18 to 20 minutes, rotating the pans once halfway through, until the cookies are a dark golden brown color. Remove the cookies from the oven, let them cool slightly on the pans, then transfer them to a wire rack to cool to room temperature.

12. Serve the cooled cookies immediately, or keep them in an airtight container at room temperature for up to 1 week.

POLISH YOUR LOOK These graham crackers also taste great when coated in dark chocolate. Simply bake them without sugar and cinnamon on top, then follow the directions to dip the cookies from Chocolate Mint Cookies (page 63) or Dipping in Chocolate (page 17).

Cinnamon Cream Cheese Sandwich Cookies

MAKES ABOUT 2 DOZEN COOKIES

Imagine taking a bite of the edge of a cheesecake, with a chunky piece of crust on your fork and a thin layer of the sweet-and-sour cream cheese filling gracing the crust. Now imagine having that flavor in a bite-size version that you can pop into your mouth by hand. These sandwich cookies are like mini inverted cheesecakes (by "inverted" I mean more crust than filling). The cream cheese icing, which adds a tanginess to the cookie, can be made with or without cinnamon.

The sugar in the cream cheese icing acts as a natural preservant, so the cookies can be left at room temperature in an airtight container for a week.

1 recipe Graham Cracker Dough (page 86)

FOR THE FILLING

4 tablespoons (½ stick) unsalted butter, at room temperature
4 ounces (one-half 8-ounce package) cream cheese, at room temperature
½ cup confectioners' sugar
½ teaspoon pure vanilla extract
½ teaspoon ground cinnamon
Pinch of salt

1. Preheat the oven to 350°F. Line two sheet pans with parchment paper or spray lightly with nonstick cooking spray.

2. Remove the dough from the refrigerator and let it sit at room temperature for about 15 minutes. (The dough should be soft enough to roll without cracking, but not yet sticky.)

3. Place the dough on a piece of parchment paper or on a lightly floured flat surface. Lightly flour the top of the disk and begin rolling the dough (see Rolling Dough, page

10). Lift and rotate the dough between each roll to prevent it from sticking. Repeat the process until the dough is between ⅛ and ¼ inch thick.

4. Using a 1½-inch round cookie cutter, cut out cookies and place them about ½ inch apart on the prepared pans. Repeat until the pans are full. (The remaining dough can be kept in the refrigerator until ready to be used.)

5. Bake for 12 to 15 minutes, rotating the pans once halfway through, until the edges of the cookies are firm. Remove the cookies from the oven, let them cool slightly on the pans, then transfer them to a wire rack to cool to room temperature.

6. While the cookies are cooling, beat the butter and cream cheese together in a standing mixer fitted with a paddle attachment on high speed until light and smooth, about 3 minutes. Add the confectioners' sugar and mix on low speed until incorporated, about 30 seconds.

7. Add the vanilla, cinnamon, and salt and mix until the icing is smooth, about 2 minutes.

8. On a separate sheet pan or work surface, place half the cookies bottom side up. Fill a pastry bag with icing (no tip necessary) and pipe about 1 teaspoon of icing onto each cookie bottom.

9. Take the remaining cookies and gently press one on top of each iced cookie, bottom side down, to form a sandwich. Allow to set at room temperature for approximately 30 minutes before serving or packaging.

10. Serve the set cookies immediately, or keep them in an airtight container at room temperature for up to 1 week.

FASHION EMERGENCY For this recipe, the Sandwich Cookies (page 58), or the S'mores Cookies (page 91), the filling can also be spread onto the bottom half of the cookies using an offset spatula. It will not be as neat or even as when you use the piping technique, but it is a good alternative if you don't have a pastry bag available.

S'mores Cookies

City dwellers, and anyone else who feels that he or she doesn't get enough time in front of a campfire, can still enjoy the taste of s'mores with these cookies, which cleverly combine the graham cracker–marshmallow–chocolate trifecta. What they lack in the crispy char of the toasted marshmallow, they more than make up for in their ability to be made in advance. They are also one of the most versatile cookies in this book as far as being appropriate for all occasions. Bring them to a family reunion, use them as a butter-up-your-boss gift, serve them with petit fours at a formal affair, or just keep them in a jar at home to treat yourself.

> 1 **recipe Graham Cracker Dough (page 86)**
> One **8-ounce jar Marshmallow Fluff**
> 1 **cup chopped milk chocolate (about 6 ounces) or milk chocolate chips**
> 1½ **teaspoons vegetable or canola oil (not necessary if tempering chocolate)**

1. Preheat the oven to 350°F. Line two sheet pans with parchment paper or spray lightly with nonstick cooking spray.

2. Remove the dough from the refrigerator and let it sit at room temperature for about 15 minutes. (The dough should be soft enough to roll without cracking, but not yet sticky.)

3. Place the dough on a piece of parchment paper or on a lightly floured flat surface. Lightly flour the top of the disk and begin rolling the dough (see Rolling Dough, page 10). Lift and rotate the dough between each roll to prevent it from sticking. Repeat the process until the dough is ⅛ to ¼ inch thick.

4. Using a 1½-inch round cookie cutter, cut out cookies and place them about ½ inch apart on the prepared pans. Repeat until the pans are full. (The remaining dough can be kept in the refrigerator until ready to be used.)

5. Bake for 12 to 15 minutes, rotating the pans once halfway through, until the edges of the cookies are firm. Remove the cookies from the oven, let them cool slightly on the pans, then transfer them to a wire rack to cool to room temperature.

6. On a separate sheet pan or work surface, place half the cookies bottom side up. Fill a pastry bag with Marshmallow Fluff (no tip necessary) and pipe about 1 teaspoon of Fluff onto each cookie bottom.

7. Take the remaining cookies and gently press one on top of each iced cookie, bottom side down, to form a sandwich.

8. Temper the chocolate (see Basic Tempered Chocolate, page 163), or heat the chocolate and vegetable oil in a bowl over a double boiler. Stir constantly with a rubber spatula or wooden spoon until the chocolate has melted. Remove the bowl from the heat and let it sit at room temperature for about 10 minutes to cool.

9. Take each cookie and dip half into the chocolate (see Dipping in Chocolate, page 17). As you remove the cookies from the chocolate, scrape one side against the rim of the bowl to remove any excess chocolate. Place the cookies on a sheet pan lined with parchment paper and allow them to set for about 45 minutes at room temperature before serving or packaging.

10. Serve the set cookies immediately, or keep them in an airtight container at room temperature for up to 1 week.

Cakes

The cakes of your dessert "wardrobe" take you beyond the everyday and into occasions that require you to be a little more dressed up, though never overdressed. The cake recipes that follow will help you prepare anything from cupcakes for a bake sale to an impressive birthday dessert for your future mother-in-law. Even the more casual baker will appreciate having one or two of these recipes in her wardrobe to try out for those special occasions.

Each of the individual recipes here is written specifically as a cake or cupcake, but all of them are completely interchangeable as far as how you want to prepare them. As a rule of thumb, a recipe that makes a three-layer 8-inch cake can be interchanged with a two-layer 9-inch cake or 30 to 36 standard cupcakes. For other cake sizes, you can use the following conversions:

* For a two-layer 6-inch cake: make one-half recipe (feeds up to 8 people)
* For a three-layer 9-inch cake: make one and a half recipes (feeds about 25 people)
* For a two-layer 12 x 18-inch sheet cake: double the recipe (feeds 40 to 50 people)

The Best-Dressed List

In addition to the specific recipes in the following chapters, the cakes and the sandwich cookies can be mixed and matched with a variety of icings and toppings. Following is a chart that shows how each of the cakes and the sandwich cookies can make everyone's "best-dressed list."

Frostings	Devil's Food	Vanilla Cake	Banana Cake	Pumpkin Cake	Pecan Cake	Carrot Cake	Sandwich Cookies
Marshmallow Icing	✳	✳	✳	✳			✳
Chocolate Icing	✳	✳	✳		✳		
Chocolate Mousse (see Individual Mud Pies)	✳		✳		✳		
Caramel Buttercream	✳	✳	✳		✳		
Basic Dark Chocolate Ganache	✳	✳	✳		✳		✳
Vanilla Icing	✳	✳					✳
"Sassy" Cinnamon Icing (see Vanilla Icing)			✳	✳	✳	✳	✳
Cookies and Cream Icing	✳						
Cream Cheese Icing	✳	✳	✳	✳	✳	✳	✳
Green Mint Icing	✳						✳
Cinnamon Cream Cheese Icing (see Cream Cheese Icing)		✳	✳	✳	✳	✳	✳
Citrus Cream Cheese Icing		✳			✳		✳
Peanut Butter Icing	✳	✳					✳
Chocolate Cream Cheese Icing	✳		✳		✳		
Raspberry Buttercream	✳	✳	✳				
Mocha Buttercream	✳	✳	✳				

Chocolate Cake

THE LITTLE BLACK DRESS

* **DEVIL'S FOOD CAKE**
* **Mini S'mores Cupcakes**
* **Rocky Road Cupcakes**
* **Individual Mud Pies**
* **Sweet-and-Salty Cake**
* **Rich Chocolate Ganache Cake**

A rich chocolate sponge cake truly is the little black dress of desserts. Chocolate cake is always a classic, equally welcome at a romantic dinner for two as at a neighborhood block party. Its versatility is illustrated throughout this chapter, as it is paired with everything from the light, fluffy Marshmallow Icing to a rich, dense Basic Dark Chocolate Ganache. The Individual Mud Pies recipe even finds a use for the leftovers or trimmings you'll accumulate each time you level cake layers for icing. Regardless of how you dress it up or down, with all its uses, Devil's Food Cake will likely become the go-to item in your dessert wardrobe.

Devil's Food Cake

MAKES ONE 3-LAYER 8-INCH CAKE, ONE 2-LAYER 9-INCH CAKE,
OR ABOUT 3 DOZEN CUPCAKES

The base recipe for our chocolate cake is the easiest cake recipe I know. It's an oil-based (as opposed to butter-based) recipe, so, just like boxed cake mixes, it can be mixed by hand in one bowl. For that reason, it is a favorite of mine to make at a vacation home or anywhere that I'm not sure about what mixers or baking equipment will be available. Once baked, this batter results in an airy, spongy cake with a rich chocolate flavor. It tends to rise a lot in the oven, especially in the center, so the cake layers will always have to be trimmed to make the layers flat before they are iced. Accordingly, be careful not to overfill the cake pans or cupcake wrappers.

3	cups all-purpose flour
1	cup unsweetened cocoa powder
2½	teaspoons baking soda
½	teaspoon salt
2	cups sugar
2	cups buttermilk
1⅓	cups vegetable or canola oil
4	large eggs, at room temperature
2	teaspoons pure vanilla extract

1. Preheat the oven to 350°F. Grease three 8-inch round cake pans with butter or nonstick cooking spray and set aside. (Alternatively, you can use two 9-inch round pans, or prepare cupcake pans or other cake pans as directed.)

2. Sift the flour, cocoa powder, baking soda, and salt into a mixing bowl and set aside.

3. Whip the sugar, buttermilk, vegetable oil, eggs, and vanilla in the bowl of a standing mixer fitted with the whisk attachment on medium speed until all the ingredients have blended together, about 30 seconds. (If a standing mixer is not available, the batter can be whisked by hand in a large mixing bowl for about 1 minute.)

4. Add approximately half the flour mixture and mix on low speed until combined, about 30 seconds. Repeat with the remaining flour mixture. Remove the bowl from the mixer and scrape down the sides and bottom of the bowl with a rubber spatula to make sure that the flour is fully incorporated.

5. Pour the batter evenly into the prepared pans. The batter should come one-third or one-half the way up the sides of the pans.

6. Bake for 40 to 45 minutes, rotating the pans once halfway through.

7. When the centers of the cakes spring back to the touch, remove the cakes from the oven and allow them to cool for 5 to 10 minutes in their pans. (You can also test for doneness by inserting a toothpick or fork into the center of the cake and checking that it comes out clean.) Run an offset spatula or dull knife between the sides of the cakes and the pans and transfer the cakes right side up to a wire rack to bring them to room temperature.

8. Once the cakes are at room temperature, ice as desired (see Icing a Cake, page 14). Uniced cakes can be wrapped in plastic wrap and refrigerated for up to 2 days before icing and serving, or frozen for up to 2 weeks. (Trim the layers flat before freezing them. Once frozen, the layers need to sit at room temperature for only 15 minutes before you start icing them, but allow 2 hours at room temperature for the cake to thaw fully before serving it.)

Mini S'mores Cupcakes

MAKES ABOUT 3 DOZEN MINI CUPCAKES

Mini cupcakes are a chic, modern-day petit four; they have become a favorite for cocktail party desserts. Although they look equally elegant passed on a tray or displayed on a table, they are more whimsical and less stuffy than traditional options, such as mini fruit tarts or truffles. At Tribeca Treats, the flavor combination of s'mores is one of our most popular: The fluffy Marshmallow Icing perfectly balances the dark chocolate cake. You can also substitute sweetened white coconut for the graham cracker crumbs and you have another great classic treat, the "Snowball."

½ **recipe Devil's Food Cake batter (page 98)**

½ **recipe Marshmallow Icing (page 140)**

½ **cup finely ground graham crackers (see Graham Cracker Dough, page 86) or store-bought crumbs**

1. Preheat the oven to 350°F. Line a mini muffin pan with paper wrappers.

2. Using a small ice cream scoop or a tablespoon measure, scoop the Devil's Food Cake batter into the prepared pan. (The batter should come halfway to two-thirds the way up the sides of the mini muffin wrappers.)

3. Bake for 12 to 15 minutes, rotating the pan once halfway through, until the centers of the cupcakes spring back to the touch.

4. Remove the cupcakes from the oven, let them cool slightly in the pan, then finish cooling them right side up on a wire rack until they reach room temperature.

5. Repeat this process to bake the remaining batter, as necessary.

6. While the cupcakes are baking and cooling, prepare the Marshmallow Icing, if you have not already done so. Set it aside.

7. Once all the cupcakes have cooled to room temperature, fit a pastry bag with a large star tip and fill it with icing. Pipe a star-shape dollop of icing on top of each cupcake (see Filling a Pastry Bag and Piping, page 11). Repeat until all the cupcakes have been iced.

8. Once iced, the cupcakes can be kept covered or in an airtight container in the refrigerator for up to 24 hours. Bring them to room temperature before serving.

9. Just before serving, generously sprinkle the graham cracker crumbs across the tops of the iced cupcakes.

POLISH YOUR LOOK This recipe will also yield 15 to 18 standard-size cupcakes or a two-layer 6-inch cake, baked accordingly. To make S'mores Cake, ice chocolate cake layers with Marshmallow Icing and gently press graham cracker crumbs against the sides (see Blueberry "Cheesecake," page 123, for instructions on adhering cookie crumbs to the sides of cake).

Rocky Road Cupcakes

MAKES ABOUT 3 DOZEN CUPCAKES

This Rocky Road Cupcake has a surprising marshmallow center that provides a yin-and-yang contrast to the dense chocolate icing. For a more daring, sweet-and-salty version, try using chopped Smokehouse almonds instead of the traditional toasted ones, or top the cupcakes with chopped salted peanuts. Once you're comfortable with the technique of filling a cupcake, you can use other fillings, such as chocolate mousse, Nutella, fruit curd, or a favorite custard, to create other flavors.

> 1 **recipe Devil's Food Cake batter (page 98)**
> 1 **recipe Chocolate Icing (page 148)**
> One **8-ounce jar Marshmallow Fluff**
> 1 **cup chopped toasted almonds**

1. Preheat the oven to 350°F. Line a cupcake pan with paper wrappers.

2. Using a standard-size ice cream scoop or a ¼ cup measure, scoop the Devil's Food Cake batter into the prepared pan. The batter should come one-third to one-half the way up the sides of the pans.

3. Bake for 20 to 22 minutes, rotating the pan once halfway through, until the centers of the cupcakes spring back to the touch.

4. Remove the cupcakes from the oven, let them cool slightly in the pan, then finish cooling them right side up on a wire rack until they reach room temperature.

5. Repeat this process to bake the remaining batter, as necessary.

6. While the cupcakes are baking and cooling, prepare the Chocolate Icing, if you have not already done so. Set it aside.

7. Once all the cupcakes have cooled to room temperature, use a paring knife to gently carve out a ½-inch-diameter column that reaches about halfway down through the

middle of each cupcake. (You can also carve this opening with a medium round piping tip by pressing the tip into the top of the cupcake about halfway down and then twisting it 360 degrees before pulling the tip out.)

8. Fill a pastry bag fitted with a medium round tip with Marshmallow Fluff. Inserting the tip of the bag into the carved center of each cupcake, pipe the filling into the cake until it just begins to overflow the cavity (see Filling a Pastry Bag and Piping, page 11).

9. Fit another pastry bag with a large star tip and fill it with Chocolate Icing. Pipe rosettes of icing on each cupcake (see Filling a Pastry Bag and Piping, page 11). Repeat until all the cupcakes have been iced.

10. Sprinkle the chopped almonds on top of the cupcakes and serve.

11. Once iced, the cupcakes can be kept covered or in an airtight container in the refrigerator for up to 2 days. Bring them to room temperature before serving.

POLISH YOUR LOOK To make Rocky Road Cake, ice chocolate cake layers with Marshmallow Icing up to the crumb coat stage (see Icing a Cake, page 14). Once the crumb coat has set, finish the cake with ½ recipe Chocolate Icing. Sprinkle almonds across the entire top of the cake or, if you're planning on inscribing it, just around the perimeter.

Individual Mud Pies

MAKES 6 INDIVIDUAL DESSERTS

Mud pies come in handy as a great use of leftovers or trimmings of chocolate cakes, cookies, or brownies. They are a great opportunity to get creative with your desserts, since there is really no "wrong" way to make them. The point is just to create a rich, gooey dessert with a crumbly crust. This particular version incorporates chocolate cake, chocolate mousse (which can also be served on its own or used to ice a cake or cupcakes), and fudge sauce. Additional toppings are limitless.

Because they are such a messy dessert, I like to prepare and offer mud pies in individual martini glasses, wineglasses, or tumblers—it makes it much easier to serve and enjoy. You can, if you prefer, fill one 9-inch pie dish, using the same method, and slice it to serve.

Cake trimmings can be collected and frozen for up to 2 months in advance, or you can bake ½ recipe Devil's Food Cake (page 98) in a 9-inch square baking pan, cut it into 1-inch cubes, and allow them to sit out and get slightly stale overnight.

FOR THE BASE

- 4 cups chocolate cake trimmings (see headnote)
- ½ cup espresso or liqueur (such as Kahlúa, Framboise, Chambord, Grand Marnier, depending on your flavor preference)

FOR THE CHOCOLATE MOUSSE

- 2 cups chilled heavy cream
- 4 large egg yolks
- 3 tablespoons sugar
- Pinch of salt
- 1 teaspoon pure vanilla extract
- 1 cup (about 6 ounces) finely chopped bittersweet chocolate

FOR THE FUDGE SAUCE

- 1 cup (about 6 ounces) finely chopped bittersweet chocolate
- ½ cup heavy cream
- 1 tablespoon light corn syrup
- 1 tablespoon unsalted butter, at room temperature

Whipped cream, fresh berries, chocolate toffee pieces, toasted coconut, or anything else you can imagine

1. Roughly chop the cake trimmings and put them in a mixing bowl with the espresso. Mash them together with a fork until the cake has completely crumbled and the liquid is evenly distributed. Set aside.

2. To make the chocolate mousse: Heat ¾ cup heavy cream in a heavy saucepan over medium heat until it just begins to simmer. While the cream is heating, whisk together the egg yolks, sugar, and salt in a mixing bowl for 1 minute, then add the hot cream in a slow stream, whisking vigorously until combined.

3. Pour the custard back into the saucepan and cook over low heat, stirring constantly with a rubber spatula or wooden spoon, until the custard registers 160°F on a kitchen thermometer. (It is important to stir constantly and scrape the bottom and sides of the pan, because you don't want the eggs to cook through and solidify. If you do notice some solids, strain the custard when you remove it from the heat.)

4. Remove the custard from the heat and pour it into a bowl. Stir in the vanilla and set aside.

5. Heat the chocolate in a bowl over a double boiler. Stir constantly with a rubber spatula or wooden spoon until the chocolate is melted. Add a large spoonful of custard to the chocolate, mix it together, then pour the chocolate into the custard, stirring constantly as you pour.

6. Whip the remaining 1¼ cups cream in a standing mixer fitted with the whisk attachment on medium-high speed until it forms firm peaks. Whisk a large spoonful of whipped cream into the chocolate custard to lighten the consistency, then gently but thoroughly fold in the remaining cream.

7. Cover the bowl with plastic wrap, and let the mousse chill in the refrigerator for at least 1 hour or overnight.

8. To make the fudge sauce: Heat the chocolate, cream, corn syrup, and butter in a bowl over a double boiler. Stir constantly with a rubber spatula or wooden spoon until the

chocolate has melted entirely and the ingredients have combined. Remove the bowl from the heat, and let the fudge sauce sit at room temperature to cool.

9. Scoop a large spoonful of cake crumbs into each of 6 serving glasses (martini glasses, wineglasses, or small tumblers work well) and press the cake with your fingers to form a dense layer over the bottom of the glass. (Save about half the crumbs to make a second layer.)

10. Distribute the chocolate mousse evenly among the 6 glasses. Shake each glass slightly so that the mousse settles.

11. Add another spoonful of cake crumbs to cover the mousse.

12. Pour the fudge sauce in a thin layer (about ¼ inch thick) to coat the crumbs, then put the glasses in the refrigerator until the dessert sets, about 30 minutes or up to 24 hours.

13. Once the dessert has set, top each with whipped cream and any other toppings you have chosen. Serve the desserts immediately or within 2 hours.

POLISH YOUR LOOK The espresso or liqueur adds another element of flavor to the dish, but for a noncaffeinated, nonalcoholic version, you can use simple syrup instead. To make the simple syrup, put ½ cup water and ½ cup sugar in a saucepan and bring to a boil over medium-high heat. Stir and continue to boil until the sugar has fully dissolved. Remove the pan from the heat and cool the syrup to room temperature before using.

Sweet-and-Salty Cake

MAKES ONE 3-LAYER 8-INCH CAKE OR ONE 2-LAYER 9-INCH CAKE

In this presentation, traditional chocolate cake is enhanced with silky-smooth Caramel Buttercream offset by crunchy, salty chocolate-covered pretzels. This flavor combination is a best seller for adult birthdays, because it's unique and sophisticated, but also made with recognizable flavors. The base of this icing is Swiss Buttercream (page 155), so it's more buttery and not as sugary sweet as traditional birthday cake icing. Flakes of sea salt just lightly sprinkled at the edges of the cake give you an extra little burst of saltiness and help enhance the flavors of the caramel and the cake. The Caramel Buttercream requires a little more work than other icings, but it's well worth the effort.

1 recipe Devil's Food Cake batter (page 98)
1 recipe Caramel Buttercream (page 159)
3 cups coarsely chopped chocolate-dipped pretzels
1 teaspoon fleur de sel or other flaky sea salt

1. Preheat the oven to 350°F. Grease three 8-inch or two 9-inch round cake pans with butter or nonstick cooking spray.

2. Pour the Devil's Food Cake batter into the prepared pans and bake as directed.

3. While the cake layers are baking and cooling, prepare the Caramel Buttercream, if you have not already done so. Set it aside.

4. Once the cakes are at room temperature (or are out of the refrigerator or freezer, if prepared in advance), ice the cakes with the caramel icing, reserving some of the icing for decorating the cake (see Icing a Cake, page 14). Don't refrigerate the cake after finishing the final coat.

5. With the cake on cardboard, a turntable, or cake plate and working over a sheet of parchment or waxed paper to catch falling pretzels, gently press the chopped pretzels, a small handful at a time, into the sides of the cake until the sides are thoroughly coated.

6. Fit a pastry bag with a medium round tip and fill it with the remaining caramel icing. Pipe dots along the perimeter of the cake top (see Filling a Pastry Bag and Piping, page 11).

7. Lightly sprinkle fleur de sel over the tops of the piped dots. Inscribe the cake, if desired, and serve it immediately, or keep it refrigerated, covered or uncovered, for up to 3 days. Bring the cake back to room temperature for about 1 hour before serving.

POLISH YOUR LOOK For something slightly more traditional, leave out the pretzels and salt and instead drizzle Caramel Sauce (page 186) over the top of the cake for a pure chocolate-caramel combination.

Rich Chocolate Ganache Cake

MAKES ONE 2-LAYER 6-INCH CAKE

With the addition of rich chocolate ganache, the Devil's Food Cake you've now mastered can go from everyday fabulous to over-the-top decadence. This recipe for a 6-inch cake is perfect for a romantic date night or a small, formal dinner party, although it can easily be doubled for a standard three-layer 8-inch cake or two-layer 9-inch cake. The ganache here has a subtle hazelnut flavor, but by simply substituting other flavorings for the hazelnut liqueur, you have a wealth of other options.

Take note: Icing your cake with ganache will be slightly more difficult than with icing because the consistency of the ganache is a bit thinner until it sets, and if it becomes too cold, it will be hard to spread. Be patient as the ganache cools. If you spread it too soon, it will be challenging to accumulate a thick enough layer on the cake. Once the ganache is spreadable (the consistency of ordinary icing or peanut butter), work quickly in icing your cake. If the ganache gets too cold and thick, it will begin to crack and pull apart the cake as you try to spread it. If that happens, just reheat the ganache over a double boiler until it becomes malleable again.

½   **recipe Devil's Food Cake batter (page 98)**
½   **recipe Basic Dark Chocolate Ganache (page 151), substituting 2 tablespoons of hazelnut liqueur, such as Frangelico, for the vanilla extract**
1½   **cups toasted chopped hazelnuts**

1. Preheat the oven to 350°F. Grease two 6-inch pans with butter or nonstick cooking spray.

2. Pour the Devil's Food Cake batter into the prepared pans and bake, as directed, adjusting the cooking time to 25 to 30 minutes for the smaller size.

3. While the cakes are cooling, bring the ganache to a workable consistency (about the consistency of peanut butter) by heating it over a double boiler and then allowing it to cool slightly, at room temperature.

4. Place the bottom cake layer over a piece of parchment or waxed paper to catch the ganache if it drips when you spread it. (You can reheat the ganache that has dripped and reuse it as desired, as long as it is free of cake crumbs.)

5. Spread the ganache about ½ inch thick onto the bottom layer and then gently press the second cake layer on top. Spread a thin layer of ganache around the sides and top of the cake as a crumb coat and let it set at room temperature. (See Icing a Cake, page 14.)

6. Once the crumb coat has set, reheat the ganache, if necessary, just until it is spreadable once again, then finish icing the cake with the ganache.

7. While the ganache is still soft enough for the hazelnuts to stick to it, gently press the hazelnuts, one small handful at a time, into the sides of the cake until it is covered. Let the cake set at room temperature for 20 to 40 minutes before serving.

8. The cake can be kept covered at room temperature for up to 2 days or in the refrigerator for up to 4 days. Bring the cake to room temperature for about 1 hour before serving.

POLISH YOUR LOOK By simply changing the flavor of the ganache, this cake can be perfect for all sorts of occasions. Here are some suggestions:

For an Asian-inspired dinner party, make the ganache with sake instead of hazelnut liqueur and sprinkle the top lightly with mixed black and toasted sesame seeds.

For anniversaries or other celebratory events, make the ganache with champagne instead of hazelnut liqueur and decorate around the perimeter of the top with rock sugar crystals.

For holiday cheer, make the ganache with peppermint extract instead of hazelnut liqueur and sprinkle with crushed candy canes.

For a not-all-chocolate version, make the ganache with Campari or Grand Marnier instead of hazelnut liqueur and use it only to fill between the two cake layers. Ice the outside with orange Citrus Cream Cheese Icing (page 146) and garnish with candied orange peel.

Vanilla Cake

THE
A-LINE SKIRT
. . . .

* **VANILLA CAKE**

* **Strawberry Vanilla Cake**

* **Peanut Butter and Jelly Cupcakes**

* **Tiramisù Cupcakes**

* **Blueberry "Cheesecake"**

While there's nothing too fancy about the A-line skirt, it's an uncomplicated favorite that flatters all figures. Similarly, an unfussy vanilla cake (or yellow cake) is always a crowd-pleaser. Vanilla is also a cake for all seasons, much as an A-line skirt can be worn in warm weather or cold.

The best part about this Vanilla Cake is that it can be easily transformed by simply stirring in additional ingredients, from fresh berries to chocolate chips, or by layering on an additional flavor, as with the espresso in the Tiramisù Cupcakes. Mix and match it with all sorts of different add-ins and icings, add a striping of jelly for extra flavor, or fill it with your favorite custard, curd, or pudding (use the same technique as Rocky Road Cupcakes; page 103). You'll find this simple favorite to be one of your most versatile staples.

Vanilla Cake

MAKES ONE 3-LAYER 8-INCH CAKE, ONE 2-LAYER 9-INCH CAKE,
OR ABOUT 3 DOZEN CUPCAKES

This is a traditional yellow cake. Pair it with Vanilla Icing (page 136), and that's about as basic as you can get, but you'll be surprised at what a buttery vanilla flavor it packs. For that reason, the Vanilla Cake/Icing combo is a favorite among both kids and adults. This cake is also a classic match for the Chocolate Icing (page 148), as well as for bolder variations, such as in the following recipes in this chapter.

2½	cups all-purpose flour
1	tablespoon baking powder
½	teaspoon salt
16	tablespoons (2 sticks) unsalted butter, at room temperature
2	cups sugar
5	large eggs, at room temperature
2	teaspoons pure vanilla extract
1¼	cups buttermilk

1. Preheat the oven to 350°F. Grease three 8-inch round cake pans with butter or nonstick cooking spray and set aside. (Alternatively, you can use two 9-inch round pans, or prepare cupcake pans, as directed.)

2. Sift the flour, baking powder, and salt into a mixing bowl and set aside.

3. Beat the butter in the bowl of a standing mixer fitted with a paddle attachment at high speed until it is light and fluffy, about 3 minutes.

4. Add the sugar and mix on medium-high speed until smooth, about 1 minute. Scrape down the sides and bottom of the bowl with a rubber spatula halfway through to ensure that the butter and sugar are well mixed.

5. Add the eggs, one at a time, mixing thoroughly after each addition. Again, scrape down the sides and bottom of the bowl to make sure that the ingredients are fully combined.

6. Add approximately half the flour mixture and mix on low speed just until the flour is incorporated, about 30 seconds. Add the vanilla and buttermilk and mix until combined, about 15 seconds.

7. Add the remaining flour and mix until combined, about 15 seconds. Remove the bowl from the mixer and scrape down the sides and bottom of the bowl with a rubber spatula to make sure that the flour is fully incorporated.

8. Pour the batter evenly into the prepared pans. The batter should come about halfway up the sides of the pans.

9. Bake for 40 to 45 minutes, rotating the pans once halfway through.

10. When the centers of the cakes spring back to the touch, remove the cakes from the oven and allow them to cool for 5 to 10 minutes in their pans. (You can also test for doneness by inserting a toothpick or fork into the center of the cake and checking that it comes out clean.) Run an offset spatula or dull knife between the sides of the cakes and the pans, and transfer the cakes right side up to a wire rack to bring them to room temperature.

11. Once the cakes are at room temperature, ice as desired (see Icing a Cake, page 14). Uniced cakes can be wrapped in plastic wrap and refrigerated for up to 2 days before icing and serving, or frozen for up to 2 weeks. (Trim the layers flat before freezing them. Once frozen, the layers need to sit at room temperature for only 15 minutes before you start icing them, but allow 2 hours at room temperature for the cake to thaw fully before serving it.)

Strawberry Vanilla Cake

MAKES ONE 3-LAYER 8-INCH CAKE OR ONE 2-LAYER 9-INCH CAKE

Fresh strawberries add an element of tartness to the simple Vanilla Cake. The thin layers of strawberry jam inside the cake further enhance that flavor. At Tribeca Treats we typically offer this cake only when strawberries are at the height of flavor, making it a mouthwatering cake for a summer birthday celebration.

> 1 **recipe Vanilla Cake batter (page 115)**
> 1 **recipe Vanilla Icing (page 136)**
> ½ **cup strawberry jam**
> 1 **cup fresh strawberries, cut to a medium dice**

1. Preheat the oven to 350°F. Grease three 8-inch round cake pans with butter or nonstick cooking spray.

2. Pour the Vanilla Cake batter into the prepared pans and bake as directed.

3. While the cake is baking and cooling, prepare the Vanilla Icing, if you have not already done so. Set it aside.

4. If necessary, trim the top of each cake layer with a serrated knife to make it even and flat.

5. Starting with the bottom layer, use an offset spatula to spread a thin layer of strawberry jam across the top of the cake.

6. Take a scoop of Vanilla Icing and spread it across the top of the jam, adding more as necessary until it makes a layer about ½ inch thick (see Icing a Cake, page 14).

7. Center another layer of cake on top of the first layer and gently press it into the icing below. Repeat the process of spreading the jam and then the icing. (Note: You might not use a full ½ cup of jam.)

8. Place the last layer of cake on top, gently pressing it into the icing, and then finish icing it with the crumb coat and final coat.

9. Arrange the diced strawberries in a ring around the top edges of the cake.

10. Serve the cake immediately, or keep refrigerated for up to 3 days. Bring the cake to room temperature for about 1 hour before serving.

Peanut Butter and Jelly Cupcakes

MAKES ABOUT 3 DOZEN CUPCAKES

Peanut Butter and Jelly is by far one of our most-asked-for cupcake flavors at the bakery. The Peanut Butter Icing is fairly thick, and it has a rich, intense peanut butter flavor, so a slightly tart jelly, such as raspberry, helps cut the richness. The composition is reminiscent of childhood's favorite sandwich, but it has a sweeter edge to it. The Peanut Butter Icing also tastes great with Devil's Food Cake (page 98) or as a filling for Sandwich Cookies (page 58).

1 recipe Vanilla Cake batter (page 115)
1 recipe Peanut Butter Icing (page 141)
1 cup raspberry jelly

1. Preheat the oven to 350°F. Line a cupcake pan with paper wrappers.

2. Using a standard-size ice cream scoop or a ¼ cup measure, scoop the Vanilla Cake batter into the prepared pan.

3. Bake for 20 to 22 minutes, rotating the pan once halfway through, until the edges of the cupcakes are golden brown and the centers of the cupcakes spring back to the touch.

4. Remove the cupcakes from the oven, let them cool slightly in the pan, then finish cooling them right side up on a wire rack until they reach room temperature.

5. Repeat this process to bake the remaining batter, as necessary.

6. While the cupcakes are baking and cooling, prepare the Peanut Butter Icing, if you have not already done so. Set it aside.

7. Once the cupcakes are at room temperature, use an offset spatula or a butter knife to spread a thin layer of raspberry jelly across the top of each cupcake. Reserve the remaining jelly.

8. Fit a pastry bag with a large star tip and fill it with Peanut Butter Icing. Pipe rosettes on each cupcake (see Filling a Pastry Bag and Piping, page 11). Repeat until all the cupcakes have been iced.

9. Using a squeeze bottle or small offset spatula, place a small dot of the remaining raspberry jelly in the middle of the top of each iced cupcake.

10. Once iced, the cupcakes can be kept covered or in an airtight container in the refrigerator for up to 2 days. Bring them to room temperature before serving.

POLISH YOUR LOOK To create a Peanut Butter and Jelly Cake, use the same technique as the Strawberry Vanilla Cake recipe (page 117) to spread the jelly between layers, and ice the cake with Peanut Butter Icing.

Tiramisù Cupcakes

This is another great example of turning the flavors you like from a traditional dessert into a more modern form. Imagine the elements of tiramisù—ladyfingers, ricotta pastry cream, cinnamon, and coffee liqueur—and figure out the components of a cupcake that will best match up with those flavors. Then, voilà!, you have a new kind of cupcake. We assemble this cupcake without alcohol, but feel free to substitute Kahlúa or another coffee liqueur for the espresso (or in addition to the espresso) to give this dessert an extra punch.

> 1 **recipe Vanilla Cake batter (page 115)**
> 1 **recipe Cream Cheese Icing (page 144)**
> ½ **cup brewed espresso**
> 2 **tablespoons ground cinnamon**

1. Preheat the oven to 350°F. Line a cupcake pan with paper wrappers.

2. Using a standard-size ice cream scoop or a ¼ cup measure, scoop the Vanilla Cake batter into the prepared pan.

3. Bake for 20 to 22 minutes, rotating the pan once halfway through, until the edges of the cupcakes are golden brown and the centers of the cupcakes spring back to the touch.

4. Remove the cupcakes from the oven, let them cool slightly in the pan, then finish cooling them right side up on a wire rack until they reach room temperature.

5. Repeat this process to bake the remaining batter, as necessary.

6. While the cupcakes are baking and cooling, prepare the Cream Cheese Icing, if you have not already done so. Set it aside.

7. Once the cupcakes are at room temperature, dip a pastry brush into the espresso and brush the coffee over the tops of the cupcakes.

8. Fit a pastry bag with a large star tip and fill it with Cream Cheese Icing. Pipe rosettes on top of each cupcake (see Filling a Pastry Bag and Piping, page 11). Repeat until all the cupcakes have been iced.

9. Sprinkle the cinnamon on the top of each cupcake.

10. Once iced, the cupcakes can be kept covered or in an airtight container in the refrigerator for up to 2 days. Bring them to room temperature before serving.

POLISH YOUR LOOK For a seasonal favorite, use this same technique to create eggnog cupcakes: Brush the tops of vanilla cupcakes with dark rum and then ice with the "Sassy" Cinnamon variation on the Vanilla Icing, page 136.

Blueberry "Cheesecake"

MAKES ONE 3-LAYER 8-INCH CAKE OR A 2-LAYER 9-INCH CAKE

This blueberry cake is a great alternative to classic cheesecake, especially in the summer, because it tastes less heavy. The Cream Cheese Icing makes this version of the cake less sweet than a typical vanilla cake. The graham cracker crumbs around the sides of the iced cake add a decorative touch, while completing the flavor and texture combination that brings cheesecake to mind. For an added element, try substituting Citrus Cream Cheese Icing (page 146) for the traditional icing.

- **1 recipe Vanilla Cake batter (page 115)**
- **1 pint fresh blueberries**
- **2 tablespoons all-purpose flour**
- **1 recipe Cream Cheese Icing (page 144)**
- **2 cups finely ground graham crackers (see Graham Cracker Dough, page 86) or store-bought crumbs**

1. Preheat the oven to 350°F. Grease three 8-inch or two 9-inch round cake pans with butter or nonstick cooking spray.

2. Pour the Vanilla Cake batter into the prepared pans and set them aside.

3. Combine the blueberries and flour in a bowl and toss the blueberries to coat. Distribute the blueberries evenly between the baking pans.

4. Bake for 40 to 45 minutes, rotating the pans once halfway through.

5. When the centers of the cakes spring back to touch, remove the cakes from the oven and allow them to cool for 5 to 10 minutes in their pans. (You can also test for doneness by inserting a toothpick or fork into the center of the cake and checking that it comes out clean.) Run an offset spatula or dull knife between the sides of the cakes and the pans, and transfer the cakes right side up onto a wire rack to bring them to room temperature.

6. While the cakes are baking and cooling, prepare the Cream Cheese Icing, if you have not already done so. Set it aside.

7. Once the cakes are at room temperature, ice the cakes with the Cream Cheese Icing (see Icing a Cake, page 14).

8. With the cake on cardboard, a turntable, or cake plate and working over a sheet of parchment or waxed paper to catch falling crumbs, gently press the graham cracker crumbs, a small handful at a time, into the sides of the cake until the sides are thoroughly coated.

9. Serve the cake immediately, or keep it refrigerated for up to 3 days. Bring the cake to room temperature for about 1 hour before serving.

Banana Cake

THE STATEMENT NECKLACE

········

* **BANANA CAKE**

* **Pumpkin Cake**

* **Pecan Spice Cupcakes**

* **Carrot Cake**

With big, bold stones and a memorable design, a statement necklace may not necessarily be a wardrobe staple, but layering a fabulous one into your outfit will surely elicit oohs and aahs. The Banana Cake and the variations in this chapter are not your everyday cakes. They are meant to be remembered. These cakes are so fabulous that your family and friends will welcome seeing them again and again.

This family of desserts is always at home for breakfast or brunch occasions, but it is really quite versatile: Serve Banana Cake at a child's monkey- or jungle-themed birthday party; serve Pumpkin Cake or Pecan Spice Cupcakes as a less-conventional Thanksgiving dessert; serve Carrot Cake at an afternoon baby shower. Once you've tasted these cakes, you won't have to look very far to find a reason to bake them.

Banana Cake

MAKES ONE 3-LAYER 8-INCH CAKE, ONE 2-LAYER 9-INCH CAKE,
OR ABOUT 3 DOZEN CUPCAKES

This cake is a less dense version of banana bread, so it can be served in many ways. At Tribeca Treats we typically serve it with Chocolate Cream Cheese Icing (page 150), but it also tastes great with Cream Cheese Icing (page 144), the "Sassy" Cinnamon variation on the Vanilla Icing (page 136), or even consider baking it in a loaf pan, cutting off a slice, and serving it alongside chocolate mousse or whipped cream and fresh berries.

The key to this recipe is to use overripe bananas. Typically, the browner the peel, the sweeter the banana has become. Since bananas are usually on the greener side in the grocery store, plan on buying them several days in advance of when you'll be making the cake. Keeping them in a closed paper bag at room temperature will speed the ripening process.

3¼ **cups all-purpose flour**

1½ **teaspoons baking soda**

½ **teaspoon salt**

12 **tablespoons (1½ sticks) unsalted butter, at room temperature**

2 **cups sugar**

3 **large eggs, at room temperature**

2 **cups mashed bananas (roughly 2–3 large bananas)**

2 **teaspoons pure vanilla extract**

1½ **cups buttermilk**

1. Preheat the oven to 350°F. Grease three 8-inch or two 9-inch round cake pans with butter or nonstick cooking spray and set aside.

2. Sift the flour, baking soda, and salt into a mixing bowl and set it aside.

3. Beat the butter in the bowl of a standing mixer fitted with a paddle attachment at high speed until it is light and fluffy, about 3 minutes.

4. Add the sugar and mix on medium-high speed until smooth, about 1 minute. Scrape down the sides and bottom of the bowl with a rubber spatula halfway through to ensure that the butter and sugar are well mixed.

5. Add the eggs, one at a time, mixing thoroughly after each addition. Again, scrape down the sides and bottom of the bowl to make sure that the ingredients have combined.

6. Add the bananas and vanilla and continue to mix until combined, about 1 minute.

7. Add approximately half the flour mixture and mix on low speed just until the flour is incorporated, about 30 seconds. Add the buttermilk and mix until combined, about 15 seconds.

8. Add the remaining flour and mix until combined, about 15 seconds. Remove the bowl from the mixer and scrape down the sides and bottom of the bowl with a rubber spatula to make sure that the flour is fully incorporated.

9. Pour the batter evenly into the prepared pans. The batter should come about halfway up the sides of the pans.

10. Bake for 40 to 45 minutes, rotating the pans once halfway through.

11. When the centers of the cakes spring back to the touch, remove the cakes from the oven and allow them to cool for 5 to 10 minutes in their pans. (You can also test for doneness by inserting a toothpick or fork into the center of the cake and checking that it comes out clean.) Run an offset spatula or dull knife between the sides of the cakes and the pans, and transfer the cakes right side up onto a wire rack to bring them to room temperature.

12. Once the cakes are at room temperature, ice as desired (see Icing a Cake, page 14). Uniced cakes can be wrapped in plastic wrap and refrigerated for up to 3 days before icing and serving, or frozen for up to 2 weeks. (Trim the layers flat before freezing them. Once frozen, the layers need to sit at room temperature for only 15 minutes before you start icing them, but allow 2 hours at room temperature for the cake to thaw fully before serving it.)

Pumpkin Cake

We serve this seasonal cake from October through December, but it's so good that people ask for it all year-round. I especially love it with the "Sassy" Cinnamon variation on the Vanilla Icing (page 136), though Cream Cheese Icing (page 144) and the Cinnamon variation on the Cream Cheese Icing (page 144) are good matches as well. Pumpkin Cake or cupcakes are a great dessert to contribute to Thanksgiving dinner, and are often a welcome variation to all the pies.

3¼	cups all-purpose flour
1½	teaspoons baking soda
1½	teaspoons ground cinnamon
½	teaspoon salt
12	tablespoons (1½ sticks) unsalted butter, at room temperature
2	cups packed light brown sugar
3	large eggs, at room temperature
2	teaspoons pure vanilla extract
2	cups pumpkin puree
1½	cups buttermilk

1. Preheat the oven to 350°F. Grease three 8-inch or two 9-inch round cake pans with butter or nonstick cooking spray and set aside.

2. Sift the flour, baking soda, cinnamon, and salt into a mixing bowl and set aside.

3. Beat the butter in the bowl of a standing mixer fitted with a paddle attachment at high speed until it is light and fluffy, about 3 minutes.

4. Add the brown sugar, crumbling it with your hands as you add it to remove any lumps, and mix on medium–high speed until smooth, about 1 minute. Scrape down the sides and bottom of the bowl with a rubber spatula halfway through to ensure that the butter and sugar are well mixed.

5. Add the eggs, one at a time, mixing thoroughly after each addition. Again, scrape down the sides and bottom of the bowl to make sure that the ingredients are combined.

6. Add approximately half the flour mixture and mix on low speed just until the flour is incorporated, about 30 seconds. Add the vanilla, pumpkin, and buttermilk, and mix until combined, about 30 seconds.

7. Add the remaining flour and mix until combined, about 15 seconds. Remove the bowl from the mixer and scrape down the sides and bottom of the bowl with a rubber spatula to make sure that the flour is fully incorporated.

8. Pour the batter evenly into the prepared pans. The batter should come about halfway up the sides of the pans.

9. Bake for 40 to 45 minutes, rotating the pans once halfway through.

10. When the centers of the cakes spring back to the touch, remove the cakes from the oven and allow them to cool for 5 to 10 minutes in their pans. (You can also test for doneness by inserting a toothpick or fork into the center of the cake and checking that it comes out clean.) Run an offset spatula or dull knife between the sides of the cakes and the pans, and transfer the cakes right side up onto a wire rack to bring them to room temperature.

11. Once the cakes are at room temperature, ice as desired (see Icing a Cake, page 14). Uniced cakes can be wrapped in plastic wrap and refrigerated for up to 3 days before icing and serving, or frozen for up to 2 weeks. (Trim the layers flat before freezing them. Once frozen, the layers need to sit at room temperature for only 15 minutes before you start icing them, but allow 2 hours at room temperature for the cake to thaw fully before serving it.)

Pecan Spice Cupcakes

MAKES ABOUT 2 DOZEN CUPCAKES OR ONE 2-LAYER 8-INCH CAKE

These cupcakes have a lighter consistency than the other cakes in this chapter. Whereas the other cakes could almost double as bread, there's no mistaking these as cake. Citrus Cream Cheese Icing (page 146) and the "Sassy" Cinnamon variation on the Vanilla Icing (page 136) are scrumptious toppings. Use the cream cheese combination for a brunch dessert or the sweeter cinnamon icing to dress them up for an autumn evening. The brown sugar and mix of spices in the batter augment the woodsy sweetness of the pecans. For a slight variation, peel and dice a sweet apple and add it to the batter before baking.

2¾	cups all-purpose flour
1½	teaspoons baking soda
1½	teaspoons baking powder
1	tablespoon ground cinnamon
1½	teaspoons ground nutmeg
1	teaspoon ginger powder
1	teaspoon salt
12	tablespoons (1½ sticks) unsalted butter, at room temperature
1½	cups packed light brown sugar
3	large eggs, at room temperature
2	teaspoons pure vanilla extract
1½	cups buttermilk
¾	cup roughly chopped pecans

1. Preheat the oven to 350°F. Line a cupcake pan with paper wrappers.

2. Sift the flour, baking soda, baking powder, cinnamon, nutmeg, ginger, and salt into a mixing bowl and set it aside.

3. Beat the butter in the bowl of a standing mixer fitted with a paddle attachment at high speed until it is light and fluffy, about 3 minutes.

4. Add the brown sugar, crumbling it with your hands as you add it to remove any lumps, and mix on medium-high speed until smooth, about 1 minute. Scrape down the sides and bottom of the bowl with a rubber spatula halfway through to ensure that the butter and sugar are well mixed.

5. Add the eggs, one at a time, mixing thoroughly after each addition. Again, scrape down the sides and bottom of the bowl to make sure that the ingredients are combined.

6. Add approximately half the flour mixture and mix on low speed just until the flour is incorporated, about 30 seconds. Add the vanilla and buttermilk and mix until combined, about 15 seconds.

7. Add the remaining flour and mix until combined, about 15 seconds. Add the pecans and mix until just incorporated. Remove the bowl from the mixer and scrape down the sides and bottom of the bowl with a rubber spatula to make sure that the flour is fully incorporated.

8. Using a standard-size ice cream scoop or a ¼ cup measure, scoop the batter into the prepared pan, so that the batter comes about halfway up the sides of the wrappers.

9. Bake for 20 to 22 minutes, rotating the pan once halfway through, until the centers of the cupcakes spring back to the touch.

10. Remove the cupcakes from the oven, let them cool slightly in the pan, then finish cooling them right side up on a wire rack until they reach room temperature.

11. Repeat this process with the remaining batter, as necessary.

12. Once the cupcakes are at room temperature, ice as desired. Once iced, the cupcakes can be kept covered or in an airtight container in the refrigerator for up to 2 days. Bring them to room temperature before serving.

Carrot Cake

Like the Devil's Food Cake recipe, this recipe is oil based, so it can easily be mixed by hand. Cake flour is used here, but not all grocery stores carry it. If necessary, you can substitute all-purpose flour—just use ¼ cup less and be very careful not to overmix the batter. Also, you'll notice that this is a raisinless carrot cake; that's a personal preference. If you want to add raisins to yours, go ahead and add 1 cup. You can also omit the pecans, particularly if nut allergies are a concern.

3	**cups cake flour**
1	**teaspoon baking powder**
½	**teaspoon baking soda**
2	**teaspoons ground cinnamon**
1	**teaspoon ginger powder**
½	**teaspoon salt**
4	**large eggs, at room temperature**
1¼	**cups vegetable or canola oil**
1¾	**cups sugar**
½	**cup whole milk**
3	**cups coarsely grated carrots**
1	**cup roughly chopped pecans**

1. Preheat the oven to 350°F. Grease three 8-inch or two 9-inch round cake pans with butter or nonstick cooking spray and set aside.

2. Sift the flour, baking powder, baking soda, cinnamon, ginger, and salt into a mixing bowl and set aside.

3. Mix the eggs, vegetable oil, sugar, and milk in the bowl of a standing mixer fitted with a paddle attachment on medium speed until they are combined, about 30 seconds. (If a standing mixer is not available, the batter can be whisked by hand in a large mixing bowl for about 1 minute.)

4. Add approximately half the flour mixture and mix on low speed just until the flour is incorporated, about 30 seconds. Repeat with the remaining flour.

5. Add the carrots and pecans and mix until just incorporated, about 15 seconds. Remove the bowl from the mixer and scrape the sides and bottom of the bowl with a rubber spatula to make sure that the flour is fully incorporated.

6. Pour the batter evenly into the prepared pans.

7. Bake for 40 to 45 minutes, rotating the pans once halfway through.

8. When the centers of the cakes spring back to the touch, remove the cakes from the oven and allow them to cool for 5 to 10 minutes in their pans. (You can also test for doneness by inserting a toothpick or fork into the center of the cake and checking that it comes out clean.) Run an offset spatula or dull knife between the sides of the cakes and the pans, and transfer the cakes right side up to a cooling rack to bring them to room temperature.

9. Once the cakes are at room temperature, ice as desired (see Icing a Cake, page 14). Uniced cakes can be wrapped in plastic wrap and refrigerated for up to 3 days before icing and serving, or frozen for up to 2 weeks. (Trim the layers flat before freezing them. Once frozen, the layers need to sit at room temperature for only 15 minutes before you start icing them, but allow 2 hours at room temperature for the cake to thaw fully before serving it.)

Vanilla Icing

THE
BALLET FLATS

....

* **VANILLA ICING**
* **Cookies and Cream Icing**
* **Marshmallow Icing**
* **Peanut Butter Icing**

Ballet flats are a simple and easy way to add a hint of femininity to any outfit. More adaptable than high heels, they are casual but classy, sweet and traditional, much like confectioners' sugar–based Vanilla Icing. Vanilla Icing is the traditional American birthday cake icing; it's what you think of when you remember the extra-sugary-sweet icing from your childhood. The sweetness of this icing makes it more difficult to pair with a wide range of flavors, but Vanilla Icing is a no-fail pairing with chocolate or vanilla cake. The icing variations in this chapter will give you additional flavor options that are equally simple to prepare.

Vanilla Icing

MAKES ENOUGH FOR ONE 3-LAYER 8-INCH CAKE, ONE 2-LAYER 9-INCH CAKE, OR ABOUT 3 DOZEN CUPCAKES

Twenty years ago this icing was more commonly made with vegetable shortening than with butter. Even now, some grocery stores and lower-end bakeries still use shortening to save money. When the frosting is made with shortening, the sugar is really the only flavor you taste. To enhance the flavors, and because of an overall avoidance of trans fats (which are common in shortening), today at high-end bakeries and at home, butter is more commonly used for the base of this icing. The secret to this simple-to-make butter icing is beating it in a mixer for a good 5 to 8 minutes total, so that it is light and fluffy.

Our recipe differs from others out there because it uses far less sugar, but this is still inherently a very sweet icing. In addition, using less sugar results in a naturally more yellow color, so if you want to get a bright white or if you're planning to tint it a different color, beat the icing in a standing mixer until it is colorless—the more air you incorporate, the whiter it will be.

To make our "Sassy" Cinnamon Icing, which pairs well with all of the cakes in the Banana Cake chapter (page 125), just add one tablespoon of ground cinnamon and mix until combined.

   1 **pound (4 sticks) unsalted butter, at room temperature**
   6 **cups confectioners' sugar**
   1 **tablespoon pure vanilla extract**
   2 **tablespoons whole milk**
     Food coloring (optional)

1. Beat the butter in the bowl of a standing mixer fitted with a paddle attachment on high speed until it is light and smooth, about 3 minutes.

2. Add the confectioners' sugar and mix on low speed until incorporated, about 2 minutes. (The mixture will be somewhat thick and pasty.)

3. Add the vanilla and milk and mix on medium-high speed until smooth, about 2 minutes.

4. Use the icing immediately, or keep it in an airtight container at room temperature for up to 3 days. Before using, beat the icing in a mixer, or stir vigorously with a rubber spatula, for about 2 minutes. Tint with food coloring, if desired.

POLISH YOUR LOOK To tint icing, add a drop at a time of your desired color, mixing primary colors as you would mix paint to achieve different colors and shades. The key is to add the color slowly and conservatively, as you can always add more color, but the only way to go lighter is to make more icing and add white. Different brands of food coloring vary in levels of intensity. The kind most frequently found in grocery stores is relatively weak and will require more drops to tint the icing. AmeriColor, a brand common to specialty cake-decorating stores, is quite intense and will yield bright colors after only a drop or two (see Resources, page 190).

Cookies and Cream Icing

MAKES ENOUGH FOR ONE 3-LAYER 8-INCH CAKE, ONE 2-LAYER 9-INCH CAKE,
OR ABOUT 3 DOZEN CUPCAKES

Cookies and Cream Icing is a serious crowd-pleaser. It's a little more distinctive than classic vanilla or chocolate icings, but it's still basic enough to appeal to traditionalists. The texture and dappled look of the icing make it easy to ice cakes with because you don't need to spend so much time smoothing the final coat. We serve it exclusively with our Devil's Food cakes or cupcakes (see pages 98–112), but feel free to pair it with any favorite cake.

> 1   **recipe Vanilla Icing (page 136)**
> 1¼ **cups finely ground chocolate cookies (see Chocolate Cookie Dough, page 54) or store-bought chocolate cookies, such as Chocolate Nilla Wafers or Chocolate Teddy Grahams**

1. Beat the Vanilla Icing in the bowl of a standing mixer fitted with a paddle attachment at medium-high speed until it is light and smooth, about 1 minute.

2. Add 1 cup of the chocolate cookie crumbs (see page 44) and mix until they have blended thoroughly into the icing, about 1 minute.

3. Use the remaining ¼ cup cookie crumbs to sprinkle on top of the iced cake or cupcakes.

4. Use the icing immediately, or keep it in an airtight container at room temperature for up to 3 days. Before using, beat the icing in a mixer, or stir vigorously with a rubber spatula, for about 2 minutes.

Marshmallow Icing

MAKES ENOUGH FOR ONE 3-LAYER 8-INCH CAKE, ONE 2-LAYER 9-INCH CAKE, OR ABOUT 3 DOZEN CUPCAKES

Although just a minor variation on the Vanilla Icing (page 136), the addition of Marshmallow Fluff makes this version a bit lighter and more smooth. The marshmallow flavor is not overwhelming, and it's a pleasant addition to the Devil's Food Cake (page 98) in the Mini S'mores Cupcakes (page 101). We also use this icing, along with sweetened white coconut, atop Devil's Food Cake and call it the "Snowball" during the winter or the "Bunny Tail" for Easter celebrations. Partnered with a smear of peanut butter, this icing is much loved on Vanilla Cake (page 115) in our "Fluffer Nutter," or substitute Banana Cake (page 126) for Vanilla in the Fluffer Nutter version to get "The Elvis." Marshmallow Icing can even be paired with Pumpkin Cake (page 128) in a dessert twist on candied yams.

> **1** **pound (4 sticks) unsalted butter, at room temperature**
> **1½** **cups confectioners' sugar**
> **2** **cups Marshmallow Fluff**

1. Beat the butter in the bowl of a standing mixer fitted with a paddle attachment on high speed until it is light and smooth, about 3 minutes.

2. Add the confectioners' sugar and mix on low speed until incorporated, about 2 minutes.

3. Add the Marshmallow Fluff and mix on medium–high speed until smooth, about 2 minutes.

4. Use the icing immediately, or keep it in an airtight container at room temperature for up to 3 days. Before using, beat the icing in a mixer, or stir vigorously with a rubber spatula, for about 2 minutes.

Peanut Butter Icing

MAKES ENOUGH FOR ONE 3-LAYER 8-INCH CAKE, ONE 2-LAYER 9-INCH CAKE,
OR ABOUT 3 DOZEN CUPCAKES

Many peanut butter icings achieve a thin, smooth consistency by diluting the peanut butter with sugar and heavy cream, but ours is concentrated and stays true to the nutty flavor. It can be more challenging to achieve a smooth finish when icing a cake with this icing, so be prepared for your cakes to have a more textured finish.

16	tablespoons (2 sticks) unsalted butter, at room temperature
3	cups creamy peanut butter
4	cups confectioners' sugar
1	teaspoon pure vanilla extract
6	tablespoons heavy cream

1. Beat the butter and peanut butter in the bowl of a standing mixer fitted with a paddle attachment on high speed until they are light and smooth, about 3 minutes.

2. Add the confectioners' sugar and mix on low speed until incorporated, about 2 minutes. (The mixture will be somewhat thick and pasty.)

3. Add the vanilla and heavy cream and mix on medium-high speed until smooth, about 2 minutes.

4. Use the icing immediately, or keep it in an airtight container at room temperature for up to three days. Before using, beat the icing in a mixer, or stir vigorously with a rubber spatula, for about 2 minutes.

FASHION EMERGENCY Some of the oils from the peanut butter may separate while the icing is stored. If that happens, just beat the icing in a standing mixer with a paddle attachment on medium-high speed until the oils combine and the icing becomes smooth again. If necessary, you can also add 1 to 2 tablespoons of heavy cream to re-smooth the icing. Additionally, peanut butter is the one food item I typically avoid buying organic, as it tends to separate more easily than traditional commercial brands.

Cream Cheese Icing

THE NAVY BLAZER
....

* **CREAM CHEESE ICING**

* **Green Mint Icing**

* **Citrus Cream Cheese Icing**

Cream Cheese Icing is the most conservative and buttoned-up of all the icings. It dresses cakes and cupcakes in a grown-up style. Unlike vanilla or chocolate icings, which create a distinct flavor atop cakes, the cream cheese really meshes with the flavor of the cake and, like a navy blazer, can be layered over almost anything. In addition, this tangy icing combines with the cake to moisten each bite, in much the same way as buttermilk softens a cake batter.

We have some customers at Tribeca Treats who may be literally addicted to our Cream Cheese Icing. They will come in twice a week and buy any and every flavor of cupcake, as long as it is topped with Cream Cheese Icing. Once you try it, you will see what a pleasing and useful icing it is, too.

Cream Cheese Icing

MAKES ENOUGH FOR ONE 3-LAYER 8-INCH CAKE, ONE 2-LAYER 9-INCH CAKE, OR ABOUT 3 DOZEN CUPCAKES

Cream Cheese Icing is a less sweet alternative to the Vanilla Icing (page 136), but it's not quite as fussy as the Swiss Buttercream (page 155), making it suitable for a Father's Day dinner or for entertaining your boss. It is also the only icing that pairs well with all the cake flavors in this book, as well as being a great filling for sandwich cookies—particularly graham crackers (see Graham Cracker Dough, page 86). (Please note: It is important that the butter and cream cheese are both at room temperature when they are mixed, or they will not fully incorporate.)

- **24 tablespoons (3 sticks) unsalted butter, at room temperature**
- **1½ pounds (three 8-ounce packages) cream cheese, at room temperature**
- **3 cups confectioners' sugar**
- **1½ teaspoons pure vanilla extract**
- **¾ teaspoon salt**

1. Beat the butter and cream cheese in the bowl of a standing mixer fitted with a paddle attachment on high speed until they are light and smooth, about 3 minutes.

2. Add the confectioners' sugar and mix on low speed until incorporated, about 1 minute.

3. Add the vanilla and salt and mix on medium–high speed until smooth, about 1 minute.

4. Use the icing immediately, or keep it in an airtight container in the refrigerator for up to 3 days. When ready to use, let the icing warm almost to room temperature.

POLISH YOUR LOOK To make the Cinnamon variation on the Cream Cheese Icing, add 2 tablespoons of ground cinnamon and mix until combined. Serve with Vanilla Cake (page 115) and sprinkle with graham cracker crumbs. It tastes like coffee cake but is appropriate for any time of day. Atop any of the cakes in the Banana Cake chapter (page 125), you'll have the perfect dessert for a New Year's Day brunch.

Green Mint Icing

Typically, I don't add food coloring to my icings unless a customer (or my daughter) requests it, but for this icing I make an exception. Just a drop or two of green food coloring makes the icing a nice shade of pale green and hints at the mint flavoring. It looks so festive atop a chocolate cupcake or mini cupcake, garnished with green sparkling sugar, that it is a natural choice for St. Patrick's Day or other springtime celebrations. The cream cheese subdues the mint essence a little, creating a softer, rather than spicy, mint flavor. Whereas the Peppermint variation on the Swiss Buttercream (page 156) is more of a seasonal option, this mint icing is popular all year long.

1   recipe Cream Cheese Icing (page 144)
3   tablespoons mint extract
      Green food coloring (optional)

1. Beat the Cream Cheese Icing in the bowl of a standing mixer fitted with a paddle attachment at medium-high speed until it is light and smooth, about 1 minute.

2. Add the mint extract and 2 drops green food coloring, if desired, and mix until the color is fully incorporated.

3. Use the icing immediately, or keep it in an airtight container in the refrigerator for up to 3 days. When ready to use, let the icing warm to almost room temperature.

Citrus Cream Cheese Icing

In this icing, the acidity of the citrus enhances the tanginess of the cream cheese. Orange, lemon, and lime all work well. Although the orange icing is my favorite, lemon is especially flavorful with fruity vanilla cakes, such as the Blueberry "Cheesecake" (page 123), and the lime icing spread over a vanilla cupcake and sprinkled with graham cracker crumbs, or sandwiched between two homemade graham crackers (see Graham Cracker Dough, page 86), can evoke a Key lime pie.

- ¾ **pound (3 sticks) unsalted butter, at room temperature**
- 1½ **pounds (three 8-ounce packages) cream cheese, at room temperature**
- 3 **cups confectioners' sugar**
- 3 **tablespoons fresh lime juice, lemon juice, or orange juice**
- 3 **tablespoons freshly grated lime, lemon, or orange zest**

1. Beat the butter and cream cheese in the bowl of a standing mixer fitted with a paddle attachment on high speed until they are light and smooth, about 3 minutes. (It is important that the butter and cream cheese are both at room temperature when they are mixed. Otherwise they will not fully incorporate and the icing will have small lumps of cream cheese.)

2. Add the confectioners' sugar and mix on low speed until incorporated, about 1 minute.

3. Add the citrus juice and citrus zest and mix on medium-high speed until smooth, about 1 minute.

4. Use the icing immediately, or keep it in an airtight container in the refrigerator for up to 3 days. When ready to use, let the icing warm almost to room temperature.

Chocolate Icing

THE
KNEE-HIGH
BOOTS

∗ **CHOCOLATE ICING**

∗ **Chocolate Cream Cheese Icing**

∗ **Basic Dark Chocolate Ganache**

Knee-high boots look stylish and chic; they can easily move from romantic and feminine to sexy and sophisticated, and they always get noticed. Likewise, a rich chocolate icing is a conspicuous part of any dessert. The silky, melt-in-your-mouth texture and intense chocolate taste are the best attributes of a sour cream–based icing. Whereas a buttercream base tends to dilute chocolate, the sour cream base heightens the true chocolate flavor, making this a sought-after recipe for chocolate lovers.

The ganache icing takes the chocolate flavor to the next level of intensity and can be enhanced with espresso or any number of liqueurs. It takes a little more finesse to ice a cake with it, because it can easily be too runny or too firm. Once you learn to recognize the right consistency, you'll pull it off every time.

Chocolate Icing

This icing is so rich and delicious that it is popular with our customers even as a "frosting shot"— straight icing eaten with a spoon. Try piping about 2 ounces into shot glasses or espresso cups and serving them (accompanied by demitasse spoons) as an unexpected cocktail party dessert. Or pull out a bowl of the icing on movie night and offer cookies and strawberries for dipping.

Just as sour cream is much softer than butter, this icing is very soft, so it's important to be flexible about the amount of sour cream you add; the amount will depend on the heat and humidity where and when you're making it. You'll add it ⅓ cup at a time at the end of the recipe, so stop adding it if the icing gets to the consistency of warm peanut butter. While not essential, for best results keep cakes and cupcakes iced with Chocolate Icing refrigerated until about 30 minutes before serving them.

For a more exotic twist, 2 tablespoons of chili powder can add a smokey heat to the icing. Try that atop Devil's Food Cake (page 98) cupcakes for a Cinco de Mayo party or other fiesta.

16 tablespoons (2 sticks) unsalted butter, at room temperature
¾ cup (about 4 ounces) finely chopped dark chocolate
⅔ cup unsweetened cocoa powder
1 tablespoon plus 1 teaspoon pure vanilla extract
4 cups confectioners' sugar
1⅓ cups sour cream

1. Heat the butter and chocolate in a bowl over a double boiler. Stir constantly with a rubber spatula or wooden spoon until the butter and chocolate are fully melted and combined.

2. Remove the bowl from the heat and add the cocoa powder and vanilla, whisking until combined.

3. Add half the confectioners' sugar and continue to whisk. (If the mixture gets too thick to whisk, you can use a spatula or spoon, but be sure to incorporate all the sugar.)

4. Add half the sour cream and mix with a rubber spatula until combined. Then add the remaining confectioners' sugar and mix until combined.

5. Begin to add the remaining sour cream, stirring constantly and adding more until you've reached a desired consistency for the icing—smooth and spreadable, like peanut butter. (If the climate is hot or humid, not all the sour cream will be necessary.)

6. Let the icing chill in the refrigerator for 20 to 30 minutes before using. The icing can be kept in an airtight container in the refrigerator for up to 4 days. Beat in a mixer or stir vigorously with a rubber spatula for about 2 minutes before using.

FASHION EMERGENCY This is a difficult icing to use for a summertime picnic or other occasions that may take place somewhere hot. If you want to use it for those occasions anyway, just keep the dessert in the shade and be prepared for the icing to get really soft. If you use the icing sparingly between cake layers, the heat won't affect the construction of your cake. Also, try using only ⅔ to 1 cup sour cream (as opposed to the 1⅓ cups called for) to make a thicker icing.

Chocolate Cream Cheese Icing

MAKES ENOUGH FOR ONE 3-LAYER 8-INCH CAKE, ONE 2-LAYER 9-INCH CAKE, OR ABOUT 3 DOZEN CUPCAKES

Admittedly, the depth of flavor of the Chocolate Icing can overwhelm some cakes. Cutting that intensity with the Cream Cheese Icing helps balance the cake and icing without compromising the flavor of the chocolate. I find the need for balance especially true with the Banana Cake (page 126). When you serve it with this Chocolate Cream Cheese Icing, you have the subtle chocolate taste, but you still get to showcase the banana.

½ **recipe Chocolate Icing (page 148)**
½ **recipe Cream Cheese Icing (page 144)**

1. Allow the Chocolate Icing to set, at least 20 to 30 minutes or overnight.

2. Keep the Cream Cheese Icing in the bowl of the standing mixer.

3. Add the Chocolate Icing to the Cream Cheese Icing and mix thoroughly until the two icings have blended and are a uniform color.

4. Use the icing immediately, or keep it in an airtight container in the refrigerator for up to 3 days. Beat in a mixer or stir vigorously with a rubber spatula for about 2 minutes before using.

POLISH YOUR LOOK To create a "Chocolate Cheesecake" cake or cupcake, ice the Devil's Food Cake (page 98) with Chocolate Cream Cheese Icing and sprinkle it with chocolate cookie crumbs (page 44).

Basic Dark Chocolate Ganache

MAKES 1 QUART—ENOUGH FOR ONE 3-LAYER 8-INCH CAKE OR 5 TO 6 DOZEN CANDIES

While the prominent taste of a ganache will always be chocolate, the essence of other ingredients will enhance the overall ganache. This recipe calls for vanilla extract, which is really imperceptible when combined with the chocolate, but it softens some of the bitterness of the dark chocolate. In place of the vanilla, any other liqueur, extract, or coffee can be added.

3¾ cups (about 1½ pounds) finely chopped dark chocolate
1 cup heavy cream
1 tablespoon unsalted butter, at room temperature
1 tablespoon pure vanilla extract

1. Place the chopped chocolate in a large heatproof mixing bowl and set aside.

2. Heat the heavy cream in a saucepan over medium heat until it is just about to boil. Pour it evenly over the chopped chocolate and let the chocolate begin to melt. Let it sit for 2 minutes. (It is important to let it sit, because if you begin stirring right away, the air you incorporate will cool the chocolate faster, making it harder for the chocolate to melt smoothly.)

3. Mix the cream and chocolate together with a rubber spatula or a whisk, working out any lumps of chocolate so that they are fully melted. Add the butter and vanilla and continue to stir.

4. If the chocolate or butter stops melting before all the lumps have dispersed, place the bowl over a pan with simmering water and continue to stir constantly until it is fully melted.

5. Set the ganache aside and let it cool before using. The ganache should be about the consistency of smooth peanut butter when it's ready to ice a cake.

6. **For cakes:** Cool the ganache almost to room temperature. Place the cake on a wire rack set over parchment or waxed paper (to catch any ganache that may drip), and ice the cake as you would with traditional icing (see Icing a Cake, page 14). If the ganache sets before you finish icing the cake, reheat it over a double boiler, then bring it down to room temperature again to finish the cake.

7. **For cupcakes:** Cool the ganache to room temperature and fill a pastry bag fitted with a large star tip. Ice the cupcakes as you would with traditional icing (see Filling a Pastry Bag and Piping, page 11). If the ganache stiffens, warm it between the palms of your hands or place it near a heated oven until it becomes pliant again.

8. **For cookies:** The ganache can be used when it's still warm, as long as it's firm enough not to drip off the edges of the cookies. Fill a pastry bag and cut a small hole (no tip necessary), then pipe about 1 teaspoon onto each cookie (see Sandwich Cookies, page 58).

9. **For truffles:** While it is still warm, pour the ganache into a prepared 8-inch square baking pan as directed in the recipe for Double Chocolate Truffles (page 172).

10. **For ice cream:** Spoon warm ganache over your favorite ice cream and serve immediately.

11. The ganache can be kept in a heatproof airtight container in the refrigerator for up to 2 weeks or frozen for up to 8 weeks. To reheat, place the container in a pan of simmering water, so that the water comes about halfway to three-quarters of the way up the sides of the container. Heat it until the sides have melted, then transfer it to a bowl and melt it fully over a double boiler.

FASHION EMERGENCY The main pitfall in preparing ganache is its tendency to "break," whereby the cocoa butter fats pull away from the rest of the mixture and refuse to emulsify. A broken ganache will result in congealed fat separated from the chocolate when it sets, a problem that is both unattractive and unpalatable. Breaking is more common with milk or white chocolate ganaches, which have a much higher percentage of cocoa butter content than dark chocolates. The easiest way to fix a broken ganache is to take half your ganache and reheat it over a double boiler until it is liquefied. Take the other half and put it in the refrigerator, so that the separated fat solidifies. Then mix the two halves together, stirring vigorously. The warm ganache will remelt the fat in the cooler ganache, and the stirring action should help it emulsify with the cream and chocolate.

Swiss Buttercream

THE RUFFLED BLOUSE
·············

* **SWISS BUTTERCREAM**

* **Raspberry Buttercream**

* **Mocha Buttercream**

* **Caramel Buttercream**

Dreamy and serene and just a tad fussy, Swiss Buttercream always "fancifies" your cakes. Classic Swiss meringue requires that you dissolve the sugar in the egg whites over heat before whipping the mixture into a meringue; this is what gives the icing the heavenly smooth quality of satin.

Swiss Buttercream is a traditional European cake icing. It has a more buttery, less sweet flavor than Vanilla Icing (page 136)—similar to what you might more often find on a wedding cake than on a birthday cake. To cut the richness of the butter, I like to use the buttercream with flavors that have some acidity or bitterness, such as lemon, raspberry, or mocha. Alternatively, play up to the richness of the icing with another buttery flavor, such as caramel.

Swiss Buttercream

MAKES ENOUGH FOR ONE 3-LAYER 8-INCH CAKE, ONE 2-LAYER 9-INCH CAKE,
OR ABOUT 3 DOZEN CUPCAKES

Swiss Buttercream is a little more time consuming to make than many of the other icings in this book because it requires a few more steps, but it is still quite simple. The slight sheen and smooth texture make it a beautiful icing to use for more formal cakes, and a bubbly, dry champagne pairs well with this icing, making it just the thing for celebratory occasions.

While useful, a candy thermometer is not required. When you are heating the egg whites, just make sure that the sugar has dissolved entirely and the mixture feels hot to the touch before you whip the egg whites to a meringue.

For best results in rebeating cold Swiss Buttercream, take about one-quarter of the icing and microwave it for 1 minute, until melted. Pour the melted icing over the cold icing, then beat it in a standing mixer fitted with a paddle attachment at high speed until it is smooth and fluffy, 3 to 5 minutes.

> ¾ **cup egg whites (about 6 large eggs)**
> 1½ **cups sugar**
> 1 **pound 2 ounces (4½ sticks) unsalted butter, at room temperature, cut into pieces**

1. Whisk the egg whites and sugar in the bowl of a standing mixer set over a pot of boiling water. Whisk constantly until the sugar has dissolved completely and the egg whites feel hot to the touch, or a thermometer reads 140°F.

2. Transfer the bowl to a standing mixer fitted with a whisk attachment and whip the egg whites on high speed until they have formed a meringue and the bowl has cooled to room temperature, 5 to 7 minutes.

3. Remove the whisk attachment and switch to a paddle attachment on the mixer. Begin adding the butter in small amounts while the mixer is on medium–high speed. (As you are adding the butter, particularly if you add it quickly, the icing may start to look as if it's curdling. This is normal. Just finish adding the butter and continue to beat the icing until it is smooth and fluffy.)

4. Once it is finished, the icing should have a smooth, shiny appearance. Flavor it as directed and use it immediately, or keep it in an airtight container in the refrigerator for up to 4 days.

POLISH YOUR LOOK For a crisp, sharp peppermint icing, add 2 tablespoons of peppermint extract, and mix well until combined. You can use it for a marvelous seasonal treat for Christmas parties, as the pristine white icing looks almost like snow atop a chocolate cupcake and then adorned with pieces of crushed candy canes.

Raspberry Buttercream

MAKES ENOUGH FOR ONE 3-LAYER 8-INCH CAKE, ONE 2-LAYER 9-INCH CAKE, OR ABOUT 3 DOZEN CUPCAKES

Pairing this icing with Devil's Food Cake (page 98) is old school, but delicious. It's what I would serve if I was catering an extravagant dinner party for my grandparents or in-laws, but it's also not out of place at a twenty-first birthday party. The raspberry icing is equally decadent with the Vanilla Cake (page 115), and it doesn't feel quite as formal as when served with chocolate. You can deepen the raspberry flavor by adding a thin layer of raspberry jelly or jam between the cake and the icing. Garnish your cake or cupcakes with fresh raspberries for an added burst of flavor.

> **1 recipe Swiss Buttercream (page 155)**
> **¼ cup raspberry puree**

1. Place the Swiss Buttercream in the bowl of a standing mixer fitted with a paddle attachment.

2. Add the raspberry puree and beat on medium-high speed for about 30 seconds.

3. Ice the cake or cupcakes as directed and garnish with fresh raspberries.

4. Use the icing immediately, or keep it in an airtight container in the refrigerator for up to 4 days. (See page 155 for a tip on rebeating cold buttercream.)

FASHION EMERGENCY It is important to use puree rather than jelly or jam to flavor the icing. The jelly will be too sweet and, once added to the Swiss Buttercream, will mask the true raspberry flavor. The unsweetened puree also produces a much more vibrant natural pink color. If you don't have frozen puree available, you can heat 1½ cups fresh or frozen raspberries in a covered saucepan for about 5 minutes. Put the raspberries in a blender to liquefy. Finally, strain well to remove the seeds. Keep any excess puree frozen for future use.

Mocha Buttercream

MAKES ENOUGH FOR ONE 3-LAYER 8-INCH CAKE, ONE 2-LAYER 9-INCH CAKE,
OR ABOUT 3 DOZEN CUPCAKES

Swiss meringue adds a lightness to traditional mocha flavor, which makes this icing a more delicate addition to chocolate desserts. To be sure to highlight the coffee flavor, use a good-quality espresso and brew it strong. If you don't have an espresso maker, go down to your local coffee shop and order two double shots of espresso to go. Also, consider a garnish of chocolate-covered espresso beans.

1 recipe Swiss Buttercream (page 155)
½ cup brewed espresso
¾ cup (about 4 ounces) finely chopped dark chocolate

1. Place the Swiss Buttercream in the bowl of a standing mixer with a paddle attachment.

2. Heat the espresso and chocolate in a bowl over a double boiler. Stir constantly with a rubber spatula or wooden spoon until the chocolate has melted and combined with the espresso. Remove the bowl from the heat, and let the mixture cool for 3 minutes.

3. Drizzle the chocolate mixture into the buttercream and beat on medium-high speed, about 1 minute.

4. Use the icing immediately, or keep it in an airtight container in the refrigerator for up to 4 days. (See page 155 for a tip on rebeating cold buttercream.)

POLISH YOUR LOOK To create a modern German chocolate cake, ice the Devil's Food Cake (page 98) with the Mocha Buttercream, top it with chopped candied pecans, and drizzle it with Caramel Sauce (page 186) for the traditional gooeyness.

Caramel Buttercream

MAKES ENOUGH FOR ONE 3-LAYER 8-INCH CAKE, ONE 2-LAYER 9-INCH CAKE,
OR ABOUT 3 DOZEN CUPCAKES

Most of the Swiss buttercream flavors we create have acidity, bitterness, or alcohol to cut the intensity of the butter, but mixing caramel with Swiss Buttercream, on the other hand, results in an extra buttery and rich icing. If you have homemade Caramel Sauce to use, then do so. The flecks of vanilla bean in the homemade caramel sauce add a nice look to the finished icing. Otherwise, you can still achieve a flavorful icing with a store-bought sauce, without the additional effort. Because the intensity of flavor may vary by brand, feel free to add a little more or less caramel, as desired. You can garnish with crushed chocolate-dipped pretzels or roasted peanuts as well as additional caramel sauce.

1 recipe Swiss Buttercream (page 155)
½ recipe Caramel Sauce (page 186) or 1 cup store-bought caramel sauce

1. Place the Swiss Buttercream in the bowl of a standing mixer fitted with a paddle attachment.

2. Warm the Caramel Sauce in a bowl over a double boiler until it liquefies, about 5 minutes.

3. Drizzle the caramel into the buttercream while beating on medium–high speed, about 1 minute.

4. Use the icing immediately, or keep it in an airtight container in the refrigerator for up to 4 days. (See page 155 for a tip on rebeating cold buttercream.)

SECTION THREE

Confections

You can go through life without ever making a chocolate truffle or confection, the same way you don't need a leather jacket or fabulous stiletto heels, but those wardrobe items are what separate the "it" girls from the girl next door. Mastering chocolate work takes some patience, but it will take your dessert repertoire from everyday to extraordinary.

Tempered Chocolate

THE STILETTO HEELS

....

* **BASIC TEMPERED CHOCOLATE**
* **Salt and Pepper Chocolate**
* **Cranberry Almond Bark**
* **Ballpark Bark**

Keeping the fat and sugar molecules aligned is an important component to working with chocolate. This is why confectioners use a process called tempering, whereby you melt the chocolate to a certain temperature, lower the temperature, and then raise the temperature slightly, in order to optimize the chocolate's molecular configuration. Properly tempered chocolate sets extremely quickly and produces a beautiful sheen on the finished product.

It sounds complicated, but with patience and practice tempering chocolate becomes quite easy. You might not get it right on the first try, but once you get a feel for tempering, you'll be able to manage it with grace. Likewise, stiletto heels can also be painful, but once you have practiced walking in them, they are hard to resist and always worth the effort.

Basic Tempered Chocolate

MAKES ABOUT 2 CUPS CHOCOLATE

Tempered chocolate solidifies easily into a hard, shiny chocolate that snaps when broken. It can be worked into a variety of shapes, spread into sheets, and used in molds. Tempering chocolate also keeps cocoa butter from rising to the surface of the chocolate and "blooming" into unsightly light brown patches.

Many chocolate experts will teach you to temper using the marble slab method: You heat your chocolate, then pour it onto a cool marble slab, stirring and working the chocolate with a bench scraper until it has cooled to the proper temperature and then returning it to your bowl. This is a beautiful, classic French method to use, but as large marble slabs aren't readily available for this purpose, here's how to use the seed method. Be sure to have an accurate digital thermometer on hand.

2 cups (about 12 ounces) finely chopped bittersweet chocolate (milk or white chocolate can also be used, as desired)

1. Melt 1½ cups of the chocolate in a bowl over a double boiler. Stir constantly with a rubber spatula or wooden spoon to ensure uniform temperature. Set the remaining ½ cup chocolate aside.

2. Once the chocolate has fully melted and reached a temperature of 105°F to 108°F (102° to 104°F for milk or white chocolate), remove it from the heat. At this temperature, all the crystals will melt and stabilize. Add the remaining chocolate that was set aside and stir. Be aware: If the chocolate rises above 120°F (118°F for milk or white chocolate), it will be unusable for tempering.

3. Stir until the chocolate's temperature cools to between 82° and 84°F (80° and 82°F for milk or white chocolate).

4. Return the bowl to the double boiler and heat slightly until the temperature is 86° to 88°F (82° to 84°F for milk or white chocolate), about 1 minute.

5. Use the chocolate as soon as possible, or keep it at this temperature over a pot of simmering water until ready to use. Be sure to continue to stir it and monitor the temperature closely. Take the chocolate off the heat if the temperature begins to rise toward 90°F (86°F for milk or white chocolate). Please note: The longer you wait to use it, the more likely the chocolate will be out of temper.

FASHION EMERGENCY Chocolate is easier to temper in larger quantities because the temperature won't fluctuate as quickly. For that reason, it is always advisable to temper more chocolate than you think you'll need. That way you won't be left short and needing to temper only a small additional quantity. Unused tempered chocolate can be poured onto a sheet pan lined with parchment paper and used for baking or re-tempering.

Salt and Pepper Chocolate

MAKES ABOUT 3 CUPS

See photograph on opposite page. Salt and Pepper Chocolate is one of our more exotic, but top-selling, flavor combinations. The idea was given to us by one of our customers, who had seen a similar chocolate bar on a trip to Paris. This surprisingly elegant flavor pairing is an eye-catching chocolate treat to set out at the end of a dinner party.

1 **cup (about 6 ounces) finely chopped bittersweet chocolate**
1 **cup (about 6 ounces) finely chopped white chocolate**
1 **tablespoon chili powder**
1 **tablespoon gray sea salt**

1. Working simultaneously but in separate bowls, temper the bittersweet and white chocolates as directed in Basic Tempered Chocolate (page 163). (You can use the same chocolate thermometer for tempering both chocolates; just wipe it thoroughly with a dry towel each time you switch bowls.)

2. Once the chocolates are tempered, take both bowls and pour the chocolates at the same time onto a sheet pan lined with parchment or waxed paper, criss-crossing them so that the bittersweet and white chocolates swirl together. Shake the pan gently to spread the chocolate (it doesn't need to be level, but it should be no more than ½ inch thick at the thickest part).

3. Sprinkle the chili powder and sea salt evenly across the surface of the chocolate. Then use a toothpick or skewer to further marbleize the chocolates and mix in the salt and chili powder.

4. Allow the chocolate to set at room temperature for 1 hour (or 30 minutes in the refrigerator).

5. Using a chef's knife or your hands, cut or break the chocolate into 2-inch shards.

6. Serve the chocolate immediately, or keep it in an airtight container at room temperature for up to 4 weeks.

Cranberry Almond Bark

MAKES ABOUT 3½ CUPS

The health benefits of dark chocolate, almonds, and dried fruit make this a great option to serve as a snack or to give as a gift to a health-conscious friend. In a box or tin beautifully tied with ribbon, the flourless bark can also make a welcome Passover hostess gift, which can be served immediately or nibbled on all week long. The dried cranberries add a delicious chewiness to this otherwise solid bark. All sorts of dried fruits and nuts can be used, but when buying the dried fruit, especially cranberries, be sure to pick an unsweetened variety. The added sugar can change the taste of the fruit and also alter the tempered chocolate.

2 cups (about 12 ounces) finely chopped bittersweet chocolate
¾ cup toasted whole almonds
¾ cup dried cranberries

1. Temper the dark chocolate as directed in Basic Tempered Chocolate (page 163).

2. Once the chocolate is tempered, pour the almonds and cranberries into the chocolate and stir with a rubber spatula until the nuts and fruit are completely coated.

3. Pour the chocolate mixture onto a sheet pan lined with parchment or waxed paper. Spread it as thinly as possible (only as thick as one layer of almonds and cranberries).

4. Allow the bark to set at room temperature for 1 hour (or 30 minutes in the refrigerator).

5. Using a chef's knife, cut the bark into bite-size pieces, about 1 inch.

6. Serve the bark immediately, or keep it in an airtight container at room temperature for up to 4 weeks.

Ballpark Bark

MAKES ABOUT 3 CUPS

Sweet and salty, crunchy and soft, this bark has all the yin-and-yang attributes of a scrumptious dessert. The peanut brittle in this recipe is also great as a stand-alone or dipped in dark chocolate. With its salty sweetness, this bark makes the perfect snack for a World Series or Super Bowl party.

FOR THE PEANUT BRITTLE

- 8 **tablespoons (1 stick) unsalted butter, at room temperature**
- ½ **cup sugar**
- **Pinch of salt**
- 1 **cup salted peanuts**

FOR THE BARK

- 3 **cups (about 18 ounces) finely chopped milk chocolate**
- ¾ **cup broken or roughly chopped pretzel bits**
- ¾ **cup mini marshmallows**

1. Lightly grease a sheet pan with nonstick cooking spray.

2. Combine the butter, sugar, and salt in a medium saucepan over high heat and bring to a boil. Continue cooking until a candy thermometer reads 300°F. Remove the saucepan from the heat and immediately add the peanuts, stirring to coat them.

3. Pour the peanut mixture onto the prepared sheet pan and spread it as thinly as possible.

4. Allow the brittle to cool to room temperature, about 1 hour.

5. Once the brittle is fully cooled, cut it into 1-inch pieces. Measure ¾ cup of brittle and set it aside, reserving the remaining brittle for another use. (The peanut brittle can be kept in an airtight container at room temperature for up to 4 weeks.)

6. Temper the milk chocolate as directed in Basic Tempered Chocolate (page 163).

7. Once the chocolate is tempered, add the ¾ cup brittle, the pretzels, and the marshmallows and stir to coat as much as possible.

8. Pour the chocolate mixture onto a sheet pan lined with parchment or waxed paper. Spread it as thinly as possible.

9. Allow the bark to set at room temperature for 1 hour (or 30 minutes in the refrigerator).

10. Using a chef's knife, cut the bark into bite-size pieces, about 1 inch.

11. Serve the bark immediately, or keep it in an airtight container at room temperature for up to 4 weeks.

Chocolate Truffles

THE LEATHER JACKET

....

* **DOUBLE CHOCOLATE TRUFFLES**

* **Wasabi–Black Sesame Truffles**

* **Ginger Truffles**

Adding a leather jacket to any outfit can give you a touch of luxury, just as adding some homemade truffles can make any dessert table more lavish. While some truffles, as well as some leather jackets, can be traditional, there is always room to include flare or edginess by adding special ingredients, such as wasabi or curry.

Truffles are actually not as hard to make as most people assume. If you let a ½- to 1-inch-thick layer of ganache set in a pan, you can then cut it into small squares—this method is much more efficient than making traditionally shaped truffles and still makes an adorable little treat. To get a round (though not spherical) shape with this method, punch out the ganache with a small (about ¾ inch in diameter) round cookie cutter instead of cutting it into squares.

Double Chocolate Truffles

MAKES ABOUT 5 TO 6 DOZEN CANDIES

These Double Chocolate Truffles are about as fundamental as you get in the world of chocolate confections. The flavor is that of pure chocolate. The vanilla extract in the ganache, combined with the milk chocolate coating, keeps this truffle from being too bitter, but the overall flavor is still closer to dark chocolate than to milk. For that reason, Double Chocolate Truffles are crowd-pleasers; they appeal to a wide range of chocolate palates. Cocoa nibs, which are roasted cocoa beans broken into small bits, give a little crunch to an otherwise silky-smooth treat and also give it a little more of an exotic or gourmet touch. Nibs can usually be found in specialty food stores, but if you can't find them, mini chocolate chips will give the truffles a similar crunch.

> **1 recipe Basic Dark Chocolate Ganache (page 151)**
>
> **FOR COATING**
> **2 cups (about 12 ounces) finely chopped milk chocolate**
> **¼ cup cocoa nibs or mini semisweet chocolate chips**

1. Line an 8- or 9-inch square baking pan or dish with parchment or waxed paper, making sure that the paper comes up at least 1 inch on two opposite sides. The paper should be smooth along the bottom and sides—any wrinkles or creases in the paper will imprint on your ganache. (A pan with sharp corners is best, but if you have only pans or dishes with rounded corners, the edges of the ganache can be trimmed.)

2. Prepare the Basic Dark Chocolate Ganache as directed, and pour it into the prepared pan. Shake it or smooth it with an offset spatula so that the ganache is flat and even. Refrigerate until set, 45 to 60 minutes.

3. Once the ganache has hardened, release it from the pan. Run a small knife or offset spatula under hot water and then run it along the sides of the pan that are not covered by paper. Turn the ganache out onto a cutting board and peel off the paper.

4. Wet a towel with very hot water and run it along the sides of a paring knife or chef's knife. Using that knife, trim any round edges from the ganache, so that you have a completely square slab. If the ganache starts to crack while you are cutting it, it is too cold, so allow it to sit at room temperature for 5 to 10 minutes.

5. Cut the ganache into ¾- to 1-inch squares, continuing to wipe your knife with the hot towel, as necessary. The key to achieving a clean cut in the ganache is a combination of making sure that the ganache is not too cold (if it cracks when you put the knife through it) and making sure that the knife is kept warm and clean so that it moves easily through the ganache.

6. Transfer the ganache squares (directly on the cutting board or placed on another plate or tray) to the refrigerator and let them chill while you prepare the coating.

7. Temper the milk chocolate as directed in Basic Tempered Chocolate (page 163).

8. Set up an assembly line of tempered chocolate, cocoa nibs, and a sheet pan lined with parchment or waxed paper.

9. Remove the ganache from the refrigerator and, working quickly so that the tempered chocolate doesn't set and the ganache doesn't get too soft, begin dipping (see Dipping in Chocolate, page 17). One at a time, using a small offset spatula or fork, dip each piece of ganache into the chocolate until it's submerged. Lift it out, shaking it gently and scraping it against the lip of the bowl to remove excess chocolate.

10. Place each chocolate on the sheet pan. Before the chocolate has set, top each with 2 or 3 cocoa nibs. Repeat until all the ganache has been dipped.

11. Allow the truffles to set at room temperature for 30 minutes (or in the refrigerator for 15 minutes) before serving.

12. The truffles can be kept in an airtight container at room temperature for up to 2 weeks.

Wasabi–Black Sesame Truffles

MAKES 5 TO 6 DOZEN CANDIES

Whereas the Double Chocolate Truffles (page 172) are the easy crowd-pleasers, Wasabi–Black Sesame Truffles should be reserved for your more adventurous friends. When mixed with chocolate, the spiciness of the wasabi is subdued, but it brings out some bitterness in the dark chocolate and gives the ganache a subtle kick. The strength of the wasabi varies greatly among the different brands of wasabi powder. Start with 1 tablespoon and then feel free to add more to taste. Keep in mind that the flavor will intensify as the ganache ages.

The black sesame seeds are an important component of the truffle, both for their texture and for their nutty sweetness, which helps balance the bitterness of the ganache. If you can't find black sesame seeds, regular sesames are a reasonable substitute, but they are a little softer and have a less intense flavor, so toast them first: Spread them in one layer on a sheet pan and roast them in a 350°F oven for 5 to 8 minutes. Check them after about 4 minutes and shake the pan gently to turn them. They should be a light to medium golden brown when they're done.

FOR THE GANACHE

- 3¾ cups (about 1½ pounds) finely chopped bittersweet chocolate
- 1 cup heavy cream
- 1 tablespoon unsalted butter, at room temperature
- 1 to 2 tablespoons wasabi powder (see headnote)

FOR COATING

- 2 cups (about 12 ounces) finely chopped bittersweet chocolate
- 1 jar black sesame seeds

1. Line an 8- or 9-inch square baking pan or dish with parchment or waxed paper, making sure that the paper comes up at least 1 inch on two opposite sides. The paper should be smooth along the bottom and sides—any wrinkles or creases in the paper will imprint on your ganache. (A pan with sharp corners is best, but if you have only pans or dishes with rounded corners, the edges of the ganache can be trimmed.)

2. Put the chopped chocolate in a large mixing bowl and set aside.

3. Heat the heavy cream in a saucepan over medium heat until the mixture is just about to boil. Pour it evenly over the chopped chocolate and let the chocolate begin to melt. Let it sit for 2 minutes. (It is important to let it sit, because if you begin stirring right away, the air you incorporate will cool the chocolate faster, making it harder for the chocolate to melt smoothly.)

4. Mix the cream and chocolate together with a rubber spatula or whisk, working out any lumps of chocolate so that they are fully melted. Add the butter and wasabi powder and continue to stir.

5. If the chocolate or butter stops melting before all the lumps have been dispersed, place the bowl over a pan with simmering water and continue to stir constantly until it is fully melted.

6. Pour the ganache into the prepared pan and shake it or smooth it with an offset spatula so that the ganache is flat and even. Refrigerate it until set, 45 to 60 minutes.

7. Once the ganache has hardened, release the ganache from the pan. Run a small knife or offset spatula under hot water, then run it along the sides of the pan that are not covered by paper. Turn the ganache out onto a cutting board and peel off the paper.

8. Wet a towel with very hot water and run it along the sides of a paring knife or chef's knife. Using that knife, trim any round edges from the ganache, so that you have a completely square slab. If the ganache starts to crack while you are cutting it, it is too cold, so allow it to sit at room temperature for 5 to 10 minutes.

9. Cut the ganache into ¾- to 1-inch squares, continuing to wipe your knife with the hot towel, as necessary. The key to achieving a clean cut in the ganache is a combination of making sure that the ganache is not too cold (if it cracks when you cut into it) and making sure that the knife is kept warm and clean so that it will move easily through the ganache.

10. Transfer the ganache squares (directly on the cutting board or placed on another plate or sheet pan) to the refrigerator and let them chill while you prepare the coating.

11. Temper the chocolate as directed in Basic Tempered Chocolate (page 163).

12. Pour the sesame seeds into a separate bowl, and set up an assembly line of tempered chocolate, sesame seeds, and a sheet pan lined with parchment or waxed paper.

13. Remove the ganache from the refrigerator and, working quickly so that the tempered chocolate doesn't set and the ganache doesn't get too soft, begin dipping (see Dipping in Chocolate, page 17). One at a time, using a small offset spatula or fork, dip each piece of ganache into the chocolate until it's submerged. Lift it out, shaking it gently and scraping it against the lip of the bowl to remove excess chocolate.

14. Place each chocolate on the sheet pan. Before the chocolate sets, sprinkle the sesame seeds over the tops of the truffles. Repeat until all the ganache has been dipped.

15. Allow the truffles to set at room temperature for 30 minutes (or in the refrigerator for 15 minutes) before serving.

16. The truffles can be kept in an airtight container at room temperature for up to 2 weeks.

POLISH YOUR LOOK For another exotic variation on these truffles, substitute curry powder for the wasabi powder and top the truffles with toasted coconut instead of the sesame seeds.

Ginger Truffles

MAKES 5 TO 6 DOZEN CANDIES

While this Ginger Truffle makes a treat appropriate for Thanksgiving and the holiday season, it's not exclusive to that time of year. With its candied ginger topping, it's a refreshing chocolate treat even in the summer months. At Tribeca Treats we sometimes offer a variation on this, adding 2 tablespoons of dark rum to the ganache, for our Dark and Stormy Truffles.

FOR THE GANACHE

- 3¾ cups (about 1½ pounds) finely chopped bittersweet chocolate
- 1 cup heavy cream
- 1 tablespoon ground ginger
- 1 tablespoon unsalted butter, at room temperature

FOR COATING

- 2 cups (about 12 ounces) finely chopped bittersweet chocolate
- ¼ cup finely chopped candied ginger

1. Line an 8- or 9-inch square baking pan or dish with parchment or waxed paper, making sure that the paper comes up at least 1 inch on two opposite sides. The paper should be smooth along the bottom and sides—any wrinkles or creases in the paper will imprint on your ganache. (A pan with sharp corners is best, but if you have only pans or dishes with rounded corners, the edges of the ganache can be trimmed.)

2. Put the chopped chocolate in a large mixing bowl and set aside.

3. Heat the heavy cream and ginger in a saucepan until the mixture is just about to boil. Pour it evenly over the chopped chocolate and let the chocolate begin to melt. Let it sit for 2 minutes. (It is important to let it sit, because if you begin stirring right away, the air you incorporate will cool the chocolate faster, making it harder for the chocolate to melt smoothly.)

4. Mix the cream and chocolate together with a rubber spatula or whisk, working out any lumps of chocolate so that they are fully melted. Add the butter and continue to stir.

5. If the chocolate or butter stops melting before all the lumps have been dispersed, place the bowl over a pan with simmering water and continue to stir constantly until it is fully melted.

6. Pour the ganache into the prepared pan and shake it or smooth it with an offset spatula so that the ganache is flat and even. Refrigerate it until set, 45 to 60 minutes.

7. Once the ganache has hardened, release it from the pan. Run a small knife or offset spatula under hot water, then run it along the sides of the pan that are not covered by paper. Turn the ganache out onto a cutting board and peel off the paper.

8. Wet a towel with very hot water and run it along the sides of a paring knife or chef's knife. Using that knife, trim any round edges from the ganache, so that you have a completely square slab. If the ganache starts to crack while you are cutting it, it is too cold, so allow it to sit at room temperature for 5 to 10 minutes.

9. Cut the ganache into ¾- to 1-inch squares, continuing to wipe your knife with the hot towel, as necessary. The key to achieving a clean cut in the ganache is a combination of making sure that the ganache is not too cold (if it cracks when you cut into it) and making sure that the knife is warm and clean so that it can move easily through the ganache.

10. Transfer the ganache squares (directly on the cutting board or placed on another plate or tray) to the refrigerator and let them chill while you temper the chocolate for dipping.

11. Temper the chocolate as directed in Basic Tempered Chocolate (page 163).

12. Set up an assembly line of tempered chocolate, candied ginger, and a sheet pan lined with parchment or waxed paper.

13. Remove the ganache from the refrigerator and, working quickly so that the tempered chocolate doesn't set and the ganache doesn't get too soft, begin dipping (see Dipping in Chocolate, page 17). One at a time, using a small offset spatula or fork, dip each piece of

ganache into the chocolate until it's submerged. Lift it out, shaking it gently and scraping it against the lip of the bowl to remove excess chocolate.

14. Place each chocolate on the sheet pan. Before the chocolate has set, top with 1 or 2 pieces of chopped candied ginger. Repeat until all the ganache has been dipped.

15. Allow the truffles to set at room temperature for 30 minutes (or in the refrigerator for 15 minutes) before serving.

16. The truffles can be kept in an airtight container at room temperature for up to 2 weeks.

Caramel

THE
"IT" BAG
....

* **CHEWY CARAMEL CANDIES**
* **Fleur de Sel Caramels**
* **Caramel Sauce**

Although an "it" bag is not the most essential item in your wardrobe, it can often give an outfit the wow factor you might be looking for. In the same way, a successful homemade caramel can be the pièce de résistance for your dessert wardrobe. Mastering your own caramel will give you another option for delectable treats suitable for anything from a lavish gift to a poker-night nibble.

Sometimes you'll splurge on one piece, like a lavish handbag, but the more you use it, the less it feels like a splurge. This caramel recipe is similar. It may take some practice to make it perfectly, but with a little patience, you'll soon be using it to fill sandwich cookies in the spring, pour over ice cream in the summer, coat apples in the fall, and give as bonbons in the winter.

Chewy Caramel Candies

MAKES 5 TO 6 DOZEN CANDIES

This caramel recipe has the right amount of butter and cream to make it nice and chewy but not too sticky. The honey and corn syrup, which also help to give it a chewy quality, are interchangeable in this recipe. If you don't have any corn syrup, you can use all honey. Likewise, if you prefer the caramel to taste less like honey, substitute more corn syrup for the honey. Be diligent in watching the candy thermometer: If you overcook caramel by just a few degrees, it will become stiff and hard to bite. Likewise, if you take it off too soon, the caramel won't be firm enough to stand on its own.

> 2¼ **cups sugar**
> 1¾ **cups heavy cream**
> ⅓ **cup honey**
> 1 **tablespoon light corn syrup**
> 1 **vanilla bean**
> 4 **tablespoons (½ stick) unsalted butter, at room temperature**

1. Line an 8- or 9-inch square baking pan or dish with parchment or waxed paper, making sure that the paper comes up at least 1 inch on two opposite sides. The paper should be smooth along the bottom and sides—any wrinkles or creases will imprint in your caramel. (A pan with sharp corners is best, but if you have only pans or dishes with rounded corners, the edges of the caramel can be trimmed.) Spray the pan lightly with nonstick cooking spray and set it aside.

2. Mix the sugar, heavy cream, honey, and corn syrup in a large pot. Scrape the seeds from the vanilla bean into the pot (reserve the pod for another use). Cover the pot and heat the mixture over medium heat for 5 minutes. (The steam that is produced inside the pot will prevent sugar from sticking to the sides of the pot and thus crystallizing your caramel. If you remove the lid and see that there is still sugar along the sides of the pot, use a damp pastry brush to wash it off the sides.)

3. Remove the cover, raise the heat to medium-high, and set a candy thermometer inside the pot. The caramel will begin to boil vigorously and, as it continues to cook, it will

become more golden in color. (If the bubbles start to rise quickly to the top of the pot, remove the pot from the heat to bring them back down. You can repeat this two or three times, if necessary, so that the caramel doesn't boil over. As the caramel reaches a higher temperature, the bubbles will subside.)

4. Cook the caramel until the temperature on the candy thermometer reads 250°F. (Be patient, but also be watchful as the caramel approaches this temperature. If it's taken off the heat a couple degrees too early, the caramel will be soft or runny. If it heats too much, it will be hard.)

5. Add the butter and remove the pot from the heat immediately. Mix the butter into the caramel with a rubber spatula until combined. Immediately pour the caramel into the prepared pan.

6. Allow it to set for at least 1 hour or overnight at room temperature before using.

7. While the caramel is setting, cut some waxed paper into 3-inch squares (about 60 to 75 pieces). Once the caramel has set, turn it out onto a cutting board and remove the paper from the bottom. Using a chef's knife or a pizza cutter, cut the caramel into approximately 1-inch squares and wrap them in the waxed paper squares, twisting the sides to close.

8. Serve the caramels immediately, or keep them at room temperature for up to 10 days.

POLISH YOUR LOOK To use this caramel as a filling for sandwich cookies, instead of cutting it into squares, use a small round cookie cutter (about ¾ inch in diameter) to punch out round pieces of caramel (excess trimmings can be reserved and used in making Caramel Sauce, page 186). Place a piece of caramel between your thumb and forefinger and pinch it to spread and flatten it to the size of a cookie (about 1½ inches in diameter and ¼ inch thick). Sandwich it between two cookies, gently pressing the cookies together. (Because the caramel is poured thick in the pan, you will want to use a cutter that is much smaller than the size of the cookie, so that you can thin it out. Alternatively, if you are planning to use the caramel only for cookie fillings, make a half batch of the caramel and let it set in the same-size pan. Then use a cutter that is the same size or only slightly smaller than the cookies to cut the caramel; there's no need to pinch it thinner.)

Fleur de Sel Caramels

MAKES 5 TO 6 DOZEN CANDIES

Caramel and sea salt has been a popular combination for gourmands for several years now, and its familiarity is growing, indicating that it's more than a passing trend. Fleur de Sel Caramels are sweet-and-salty bonbons that can be served at any time of the year. Not as dainty as the chocolate truffles, they can blend in easily at a more casual affair. Fleur de sel is fairly easy to find at specialty food stores nowadays, and also is not uncommon at many grocery stores. It and other flaky sea salts have a less salty taste than processed salts, so their delicate quality won't overwhelm the caramel and chocolate here.

1 **recipe Chewy Caramel Candies (page 182)**
2 **cups (about 12 ounces) finely chopped dark chocolate**
2 **tablespoons fleur de sel (or other flaky sea salt)**

1. Slice the Chewy Caramel Candies into squares as directed and set aside.

2. Temper the chocolate as directed in Basic Tempered Chocolate (page 163).

3. Set up an assembly line of tempered chocolate, fleur de sel, and a sheet pan lined with parchment or waxed paper.

4. Working quickly so that the tempered chocolate doesn't set, begin dipping (see Dipping in Chocolate, page 17).

5. One at a time, using a small offset spatula or fork, dip each piece of caramel into the chocolate until it's submerged. Lift it out, shaking it gently and scraping it against the lip of the bowl to remove excess chocolate.

6. Place each caramel on the sheet pan. Before the chocolate has set, sprinkle lightly with fleur de sel. Repeat until all the caramel has been dipped and sprinkled.

7. Allow the candies to set at room temperature for 30 minutes before serving. Do not refrigerate them because the caramel will harden.

8. The candies can be kept in an airtight container at room temperature for up to 2 weeks.

Caramel Sauce

With real vanilla bean and honey, homemade caramel sauce will have a much more expressive flavor than anything store bought. This recipe is a great use for leftover caramel—if you have any scraps after cutting Chewy Caramel Candies or if you make more than you need (see Fashion Emergency below). Drizzling the sauce over ice cream is the obvious use, but the sauce can also add an extra element of flavor when served as a topping on cupcakes or a cake.

¾ **cup heavy cream**
1½ **cups Chewy Caramel Candies (page 182)**

1. Heat the heavy cream in a saucepan over medium-high heat until it reaches a simmer.

2. Add the Chewy Caramel Candies, stirring constantly until they have melted and combined with the cream.

3. Serve the sauce immediately, or keep it in an airtight container at room temperature for 1 week. The caramel sauce should not harden when stored, but it will be easier to pour or spoon out if you reheat it. To reheat, simmer a pot of water and place the container with the caramel in the water (make sure that the water goes only about three-quarters the way up the side of the container). Heat it until the caramel liquefies. If you are drizzling it on top of icing, allow the caramel to cool for 5 to 10 minutes before using.

FASHION EMERGENCY If you want to make caramel sauce but don't have the caramel candies already made, just make half the recipe for Chewy Caramel Candies, but double the amount of heavy cream and cook to only 240°F. Allow the sauce to cool in the pot to a usable temperature before serving or keeping in an airtight container.

POLISH YOUR LOOK Following are some ideas for incorporating Caramel Sauce into your cake and cupcake presentations:

For Dulce de Leche, drizzle Caramel Sauce over Vanilla Cake (page 115), topped with Caramel Buttercream (page 159).

For German Chocolate Cake, top Devil's Food Cake (page 98) with Mocha Buttercream (page 158) and candied pecans and a drizzle of Caramel Sauce.

Add Caramel Sauce to the Sweet-and-Salty Cake (page 108) for extra decadence. Spoon Caramel Sauce over slices of Devil's Food Cake (page 98) topped with Chocolate Icing (page 148).

Acknowledgments

First and foremost, thank you to all of our Tribeca Treats customers. Your loyalty and support make it possible for me to do what I love every day. Thanks also to all the staff at Tribeca Treats. Special thanks to Laura Werts: Your hard work, enthusiasm, and creativity make it truly fun to come to work. Most especially, to Michele O'Hara, thank you for your loyalty: Without you I literally would have never found time to get this done.

Thanks to everyone at Random House, especially my editor, Pamela Cannon, who saw the potential in me and my idea, as only a fellow Colgate grad could. Thanks to Porscha Burke, for testing recipes, answering questions, and generally providing moral and logistical support. Thanks to Ben Fink for all your photographic talent.

To my agent, Laura Nolan, who was on board with my idea before it was even fully formed, thanks for your advice and advocacy. Thanks to my publicists, Sarah Hall and Cristina Dennstedt, and everyone else at Sarah Hall Productions, who have supported Tribeca Treats from the very beginning.

To my many friends who have offered their professional advice or services for free, including Matt Lipson, Dave Schwarz, Jesse Lutz, Elisa Strauss, Cara Gorman, Megan Frank, Liz and Chris Marsh, Zach Perles, and Marshall Phelps. You are all not only fun but incredibly creative people.

Thanks to my entire family, immediate and extended, Schifters, Doars, and Thebaults, for all the support you have given me emotionally and financially. Special thanks to recipe-testing cousins, Maggie Walsh and Maddie Doar. Extra special thanks to my parents and my sisters Danni and Laura. And to my youngest sister, Cassie, thank you for helping me and Tribeca Treats with more than I can even list on one page.

Finally, thank you, Robin. I can't even put into words what I owe you.

So many people have helped me out along the way—if I didn't mention you individually, please don't take offense. I am truly blessed with my network of friendship and support.

Resources

Kitchen Equipment and Bakeware

ATECO www.atecousa.com; 800-645-7170

BED BATH & BEYOND www.bedbathandbeyond.com; 800-462-3966

BROADWAY PANHANDLER www.broadwaypanhandler.com; 212-966-3434, 866-266-5927

JB PRINCE www.jbprince.com; 212-683-3553, 800-683-3553

SUR LA TABLE www.surlatable.com; 800-243-0852

WILLIAMS-SONOMA www.williams-sonoma.com; 877-812-6235

Cake Decorating Supplies

N.Y. CAKE & BAKING DISTRIBUTOR www.nycake.com; 212-675-2253, 877-692-2583

PFEIL & HOLING www.cakedeco.com; 718-545-4600, 800-247-7955

WILTON www.wilton.com; 800-794-5866

Chocolate-Making Supplies

AMERICAN CHOCOLATE DESIGNS www.americanchocolatedesigns.com; 877-442-3682

CHOCOVISION www.chocovision.com; 800-324-6252

Specialty Ingredients

AMERICOLOR www.americolorcorp.com; 800-556-0233

THE CHEFS' WAREHOUSE www.chefswarehouse.com; 718-842-8700

DURKEE-MOWER www.marshmallowfluff.com; 781-593-8007

INDIA TREE www.indiatree.com; 800-369-4848

WHOLE FOODS www.wholefoodsmarket.com

Packaging and Other Supplies

THE CONTAINER STORE www.containerstore.com; 888-266-8246

NASHVILLE WRAPS www.nashvillewraps.com; 800-547-9727

Index

Page numbers in *italics* refer to illustrations.

A

Almond Bark, Cranberry, *166,* 167
Amaretto Chocolate Thumbprints,
    38–39

B

baking powder, 1–2
baking soda, 1–2
Ballpark Bark, 168–69, *169*
Banana Cake, 125, 126–27
Basic Dark Chocolate Ganache,
    151–53
basics, 1–19
    basic techniques, 8–18
    essential equipment, 4–8
    major ingredients, 1–4
Basic Tempered Chocolate,
    163–64, *164*
Black and White Cookies, Mini,
    77–78, *79*
Black Sesame–Wasabi Truffles,
    174–75, *176,* 177
Blueberry "Cheesecake,"
    123–24, *124*
brownies, 66–68, *69, 70,* 71–75
    Fudgy, 67–68, *69*
    Mint Swirl, 74–75
    Peanut Butter, 72–73
    Sundae Parfait, *70,* 71
Brownie Sundae Parfait, *70,* 71
brushes, 4

butter, 2
    creaming, 10
buttercream, 154–59
    Caramel, 159
    Mocha, 158
    Raspberry, 157
    Swiss, 155–56, *156*
buttermilk, 3
buttermilk cookies, 76–78, *79,*
    80–83
    Cinnamon-Glazed Tea,
        82–83
    Lime-Glazed Tea, 80–81
    Mini Black and White, 77–78, *79*

C

cake(s), 95–159
    Banana, 125, 126–27
    Blueberry "Cheesecake," 123–24,
        124
    Carrot, 132, *133,* 134
    chocolate, 97–99, *100,* 101–104,
        104, 105–107, *107,* 108, *109,*
        110–112
    conversions, 96
    Devil's Food, 98–99
    icings, *13, 14–15, 15,* 16,
        135–59
    Individual Mud Pies, 105–7, *107*
    Mini S'mores Cupcakes, *100,*
        101–2

Peanut Butter and Jelly Cupcakes,
    119–20
Pecan Spice Cupcakes, 130–31
Pumpkin, 128–29
Rich Chocolate Ganache,
    111–12
Rocky Road Cupcakes, 103–4,
    104
Strawberry Vanilla, 117–18, *118*
Sweet-and-Salty, 108, *109,* 110
Tiramisù Cupcakes, 121–22
vanilla, 113, *114,* 115–18, *118,*
    119–24, *124*
Vanilla, 115–16
cake pans, 4–5
cake turntable, 5
candy thermometer, 5
caramel, 181–83, *184,* 185–86, *187*
    Chewy Caramel Candies,
        182–83
    Fleur de Sel, *184,* 185
    Sauce, 186–87, *187*
Caramel Buttercream, 159
Caramel Sauce, 186–87, *187*
Carrot Cake, 132, *133,* 134
"Cheesecake," Blueberry,
    123–24, *124*
Chewy Caramel Candies, 182–83
chocolate, 2
    Ballpark Bark, 168–69, *169*
    Basic Tempered, 163–64, *164*

chocolate *(cont.)*
Brownie Sundae Parfait, *70,* 71
Chocolate Amaretto
Thumbprints, 38–39
Chocolate Chip Cookies, 24–25
Chocolate Cookie Dough, 54–55
Chocolate Mint Cookies, 63–65
Cookie Sticks with Fondue,
56–57, *57*
Cranberry Almond Bark, *166,*
167
Devil's Food Cake, 98–99
dipping, *17,* 17–18
Double Chocolate Truffles,
172–73
Fleur de Sel Caramels, *184,* 185
Fudgy Brownies, 67–68, *69*
Ginger Truffles, 178–80
Ice Cream Sandwiches, 60, *61,* 62
icing, 147–53
Individual Mud Pies, 105–7, *107*
Mini S'mores Cupcakes, *100,*
101–2
Mint Swirl Brownies, 74–75
Peanut Butter Brownies, 72–73
Peanut Butter and Chocolate
Thumbprints, 34–35
Rich Chocolate Ganache Cake,
111–12
Rocky Road Cupcakes,
103–104, *104*
Salt and Pepper, *164,* 165
Sandwich Cookies, 58–59, *59*
S'mores Cookies, 91–92, *92*
Sweet-and-Salty Cake, 108,
109, 110
tempered, 162–64, *164,* 165, *166,*
167–69
Wasabi–Black Sesame Truffles,
174–75, *176,* 177
White Chocolate Coconut
Cookies, 26–27
Chocolate Amaretto Thumbprints,
38–39
chocolate cake, 97–99, *100,* 101–4,
104, 105–7, *107,* 108, *109,*
110–12

Devil's Food, 98–99
Individual Mud Pies, 105–7, *107*
Mini S'mores Cupcakes, *100,*
101–2
Rich Chocolate Ganache, 111–12
Rocky Road Cupcakes, 103–4,
104
Sweet-and-Salty, 108, *109,* 110
Chocolate Chip Cookies, 24–25
chocolate cookies, 53–57, *57,* 58–59,
59, 60, *61,* 62–65
Chocolate Mint Cookies, 63–65
Dough, 54–55
Ice Cream Sandwiches, 60, *61,* 62
Sandwich Cookies, 58–59, *60*
Sticks with Fondue, 56–57, *57*
Chocolate Cookie Sticks with
Fondue, 56–57, *57*
Chocolate Cream Cheese Icing, 150
chocolate icing, 147–53
Basic Dark Chocolate Ganache,
151–53
Chocolate, 148–49, *149*
Cream Cheese, 150
Chocolate Icing, 148–49, *149*
Chocolate Mint Cookies, 63–65
chocolate truffles, *170,* 171–75, *176,*
177–80
Double Chocolate, 172–73
Ginger Truffles, 178–80
Wasabi–Black Sesame, 174–75,
176, 177
cinnamon:
Cinnamon Cream Cheese
Sandwich Cookies, 89–90
Cinnamon-Glazed Tea Cookies,
82–83
Snickerdoodles, 30–31
Cinnamon Cream Cheese Sandwich
Cookies, 89–90
Cinnamon-Glazed Tea Cookies,
82–83
Citrus Cream Cheese Icing, 146
cocoa powder, 2
Coconut White Chocolate Cookies,
26–27
confections, 160–87

Ballpark Bark, 168–69, *169*
Basic Tempered Chocolate,
163–64, *164*
caramel, 181–83, *184,*
185–87, *187*
Cranberry Almond Bark,
166, 167
Double Chocolate Truffles,
172–73
Ginger Truffles, 178–80
Salt and Pepper Chocolate,
164, 165
Wasabi–Black Sesame Truffles,
174–75, *176,* 177
cookie(s), 29–93
brownies, 66–68, *69, 70,* 71–75
Brownie Sundae Parfait, *70,* 71
buttermilk, 76–78, *79,* 80–83
chocolate, 53–57, *57,* 58–59, *59,*
60, *61,* 62–65
Chocolate Amaretto
Thumbprints, 38–39
Chocolate Chip, 24–25
Chocolate Cookie Dough, 54–55
Chocolate Cookie Sticks with
Fondue, 56–57, *57*
Chocolate Mint, 63–65
Cinnamon Cream Cheese
Sandwich Cookies, 89–90
Cinnamon-Glazed Tea, 82–83
Decorated Sugar, 43–44, *45*
Fudgy Brownies, 67–68, *69*
Graham Cracker Dough, *85,*
86–88
graham crackers, 84, *85,*
86–92, *93*
Ice Cream Sandwiches, 60, *61,* 62
icing, 12
Lime-Glazed Tea, 80–81
Linzer Thumbprints, 36–37
Mini Black and White, 77–78, *79*
Mint Swirl Brownies, 74–75
Oatmeal Raisin, 28–29
Peanut Butter and Chocolate
Thumbprints, 34–35
Peanut Butter Brownies, 72–73
Royal Icing, 49–50, *51,* 52

Sandwich, 58–59, *59*
scooped, 22, 23–31
S'mores, 91–92, *92*
Snickerdoodles, 30–31
Strawberry "Shortcakes,"
    46, *47–48*
thumbprint, *32,* 33–39
vanilla, 40–44, *45–46, 47–50,*
    51, 52
Vanilla Cookie Dough, 41–42
White Chocolate Coconut,
    26–27
Cookies and Cream Icing, *138,* 139
Cranberry Almond Bark, *166,* 167
cream, 3
Cream Cheese Cinnamon Sandwich
    Cookies, 89–90
cream cheese icing, 143–46
    Chocolate, 150
    Citrus, 146
    Cream Cheese, 144
    Green Mint, 145
Cream Cheese Icing, 144
cupcake(s):
    icing, 14, 135–59
    Mini S'mores, *100,* 101–2
    Peanut Butter and Jelly, 119–20
    Pecan Spice, 130–31
    Rocky Road, 103–4, *104*
    Tiramisù, 121–22

D
dairy, 2–3
Dark Chocolate Ganache, Basic,
    151–53
Decorated Sugar Cookies,
    43–44, *45*
Devil's Food Cake, 98–99
dipping chocolate, *17,* 17–18
double boiling, 16
Double Chocolate Truffles, 172–73
dough, rolling, 10–11

E
eggs, 3
equipment, essential, 4–8
extracts, 3–4

F
Fleur de Sel Caramels, *184,* 185
flour, 3
    all-purpose vs. cake, 3
    sifting, 9
Fondue, Chocolate Cookie Sticks
    with, 56–57, *57*
freezing, 19
Fudgy Brownies, 67–68, *69*

G
Ganache, Basic Dark Chocolate,
    151–53
Ganache Cake, Rich Chocolate,
    111–12
Ginger Truffles, 178–80
Graham Cracker Dough, *85,* 86–88
graham crackers, 84, *85,* 86–92, *93*
    Cinnamon Cream Cheese
        Sandwich Cookies, 89–90
    Dough, *85,* 86–88
    Mini S'mores Cupcakes, *100,*
        101–2
    S'mores Cookies, 91–92, *92*
Green Mint Icing, 145

H
hazelnuts:
    Linzer Thumbprints, 36–37

I
Ice Cream Sandwiches, 60, *61,* 62
ice cream scoops, 5
icing, 11–16, 135–59
    Caramel Buttercream, 158
    chocolate, 147–53
    Chocolate, 148–49, *149*
    Chocolate Cream Cheese, 150
    Citrus Cream Cheese, 146
    Cookies and Cream, *138,* 139
    cream cheese, 143–46
    Cream Cheese, 144
    Green Mint, 145
    Marshmallow, 140
    Mocha Buttercream, 159
    pastry bag filling and piping,
        11–14

Peanut Butter, 141
    Raspberry Buttercream, 157
    Royal Icing Cookies, 49–50,
        51, 52
    Swiss Buttercream, 155–56, *156*
    techniques, 11–12, *13,* 14–15,
        15, 16
    Vanilla, 135, 136–37
Individual Mud Pies, 105–7, *107*
ingredients, major, 1–4

K
knives, 6

L
Lime-Glazed Tea Cookies, 80–81
Linzer Thumbprints, 36–37

M
marshmallow:
    Icing, 140
    Mini S'mores Cupcakes, *100,*
        101–2
    Rocky Road Cupcakes,
        103–4, *104*
    S'mores Cookies, 91–92, *92*
Marshmallow Icing, 140milk, 3
Mini Black and White Cookies,
    77–78, *79*
Mini S'mores Cupcakes, *100,*
    101–2
Mint Chocolate Cookies, 63–65
Mint Icing, Green, 145
Mint Swirl Brownies, 74–75
mise en place, 8–9
Mocha Buttercream, 158
Mud Pies, Individual, 105–7, *107*

O
Oatmeal Raisin Cookies, 28–29
offset spatula, 6

P
parchment paper, 6
Parfait, Brownie Sundae, *70,* 71
pastry bags and tips, 6–7
    filling and piping, 11–14

peanut butter:
    Brownies, 72–73
    Icing, 141
    Peanut Butter and Chocolate
        Thumbprints, 34–35
    Peanut Butter and Jelly Cupcakes,
        119–20
Peanut Butter and Chocolate
    Thumbprints, 34–35
Peanut Butter and Jelly Cupcakes,
    119–20
Peanut Butter Brownies, 72–73
Peanut Butter Icing, 141
peanuts:
    Ballpark Bark, 168–69, *169*
Pecan Spice Cupcakes, 130–31
piping, 11–14
Pumpkin Cake, 128–29

R

Raisin Oatmeal Cookies, 28–29
Rich Chocolate Ganache Cake,
    111–12
Rocky Road Cupcakes, 103–4, *104*
rolling dough, 10–11
rolling pins, 7
royal icing, 12–14
Royal Icing Cookies, 49–50, *51,* 52
rubber spatula, 7

S

Salt and Pepper Chocolate, *164,* 165
Sandwich Cookies, 58–59, *59*
    Cinnamon Cream Cheese,
        89–90
Sandwiches, Ice Cream, 60, *61,* 62
scooped cookies, *22,* 23–31
    Chocolate Chip Cookies, 24–25
    Oatmeal Raisin Cookies, 28–29
    Snickerdoodles, 30–31

White Chocolate Coconut
    Cookies, 26–27
sheet pans, 7
S'mores Cookies, 91–92, *92*
S'mores Cupcakes, Mini, *100,*
    101–2
Snickerdoodles, 30–31
Spice Cupcakes, Pecan, 130–31
squeeze bottles, 7–8
standing mixer, 8
strawberry:
    "Shortcakes," *46,* 47–48
    Vanilla Cake, 117–18, *118*
Strawberry "Shortcakes," *46,* 47–48
Strawberry Vanilla Cake, 117–18, *118*
Sugar Cookies, Decorated, 43–44, *45*
Sweet-and-Salty Cake, 108, *109,* 110
Swiss buttercream, 154–59
    Caramel, 159
    Mocha, 158
    Raspberry, 157
    Swiss Buttercream, 155–56, *156*

T

Tea Cookies, Cinnamon-Glazed,
    82–83
Tea Cookies, Lime-Glazed, 80–81
techniques, basic, 8–18
tempered chocolate, 162–64, *164,*
    165–67, *167,* 168
    Ballpark Bark, 168–69, *169*
    Basic, 163–64, *164*
    Cranberry Almond Bark, *166,*
        167
    Salt and Pepper, 165
thumbprint cookies, *32,* 33–39
    Chocolate Amaretto, 38–39
    Linzer, 36–37
    Peanut Butter and Chocolate,
        34–35

Tiramisù Cupcakes, 121–22
truffles, *170,* 171–80
    chocolate, *170,* 171–75, *176,*
        177–80
    Double Chocolate, 172–73
    Ginger, 178–80
    Wasabi–Black Sesame, 174–75,
        176, 177

V

vanilla, 3–4
    Icing, 135, 136–37
vanilla cake, 113, *114,* 115–18, *118,*
    119–24, *124*
    Blueberry "Cheesecake,"
        123–24, *124*
    Peanut Butter and Jelly Cupcakes,
        119–20
    Strawberry, 117–18, *118*
    Tiramisù Cupcakes, 121–22
    Vanilla Cake, 115–16
Vanilla Cake, 115–16
vanilla cookies, 40–44, *45–46,*
    47–50, *51,* 52
    Decorated Sugar Cookies,
        43–44, *45*
    Dough, 41–42
    Royal Icing Cookies, 49–50,
        51, 52
    Strawberry "Shortcakes,"
        46, 47–48
Vanilla Icing, 135, 136–37

W

Wasabi–Black Sesame Truffles,
    174–75, *176,* 177
White Chocolate Coconut Cookies,
    26–27

About the Author

....

RACHEL SCHIFTER THEBAULT, owner and head confectioner of Tribeca Treats, spent seven years as an investment banker before transforming her hobby of making truffles for friends into a full-time career in confections. A graduate of the Institute of Culinary Education, she opened the Tribeca Treats retail store in 2007. The bakery has won honors from American Express OPEN and entrepreneur organizations, and is a pillar of the Tribeca community. A sought-after speaker and panelist, she also frequently teaches cooking and baking to children. She currently lives in Tribeca (and travels the globe) with her husband and their two daughters.